HEAVEN

HEAVEN

DAVID B. SMITH

REVIEW AND HERALD® PUBLISHING ASSOCIATION
HAGERSTOWN, MD 21740

The author assumes full responsibility for the accuracy of all facts and quotations as cited in this book.

This book was
Edited by Lawrence Maxwell
Designed by Byron Steele
Cover photo by Comstock, Inc.
Type set: 11/12 Korinna

PRINTED IN U.S.A.

95 94 93 92 91   10 9 8 7 6 5 4 3 2 1

Library of Congress Cataloging in Publication Data
Smith, David B.
  Heaven / David B. Smith.
    p. cm.
  1. Heaven. I. Title.
BT846.2S583   1991
236'.24—dc20   90-22586
                                                              CIP

ISBN 0-8280-0607-5

DEDICATION

This book is gratefully dedicated to great preachers everywhere who proclaim the living reality of heaven. Three, in particular, have touched my life.

My grandfather, Elder Daniel Venden, who for some 50 years preached with conviction about the second coming of Jesus and the urgency of choosing a heaven-bound life.

My uncle, Dr. Morris Venden, whose Spirit-filled books helped show me how to get there.

And my dad, Elder Kenneth Smith, whose dedicated life of mission service and personal example gave me incentive to go.

CONTENTS

FOREWORD

In the dedication to this book, I mentioned my Uncle Morris. A childhood memory he once shared with me epitomizes why I decided to write *Heaven*.

Morris's dad, Melvin Venden, who was an old-time evangelistic preacher (my family tree is full of 'em), suggested at worship one evening that each member of the family describe his or her dream home in heaven. Morris sat up eagerly.

"Do I get to have my own place in heaven, Dad?"

His father smiled. "Don't you want to live with Mom and me up there, Morris?"

"Nope. I want to have a house all to myself."

Dad nodded. "Sure, you can have your own place. Why don't you tell us about it?"

The beaming lad waxed eloquent, his boyhood mansion bursting at the seams with all sorts of childish dreams-come-true. The family listened patiently.

Next his older brother, Louis, described his anticipated mansion. Then Mom.

Finally my great-uncle Melvin began to speak, slowly at first, and then with an animation and eloquence born of years of heartfelt gospel preaching. He poured a devoted dad's heart into a vivid description that left both boys agog, their mouths hanging open in envy.

Finally he finished the breathtaking portrait, ". . . and *that's* my mansion. What do you think?"

A silence hung in the air. Finally Morris spoke up, reluctantly. "Dad . . . is it OK if I come live with you?"

* * *

Real mansions. Really *nice* mansions. In fact, really nice everything. I want to write . . . and pray . . . and think . . . and share . . . the reality of heaven.

Heaven is a real place, and we are going there soon! I'd like to be among the group of Christians who share this great

9

last-day message with the world.

Real. And soon. Very soon, now.

* * *

Recently I toured the Holy Land with a group of fellow Christians. The week was a blur of inspiring moments; the last day stands out in particular.

On that final Tuesday, we visited two different tombs where it is suggested that Jesus was buried. At the second one we went to—the garden tomb—our group celebrated Communion together. Quietly, prayerfully, near the very spot where many believe Christ rested during Crucifixion weekend, we worshiped, imagining the scenes of that Friday afternoon.

I stood there alone, later, tears standing in my eyes while I reflected on those momentous events of 2,000 years ago. I had to admit to myself that we could not be sure this was the very spot where they all happened. It felt right; I could imagine our Saviour lying in this tomb so restfully, His mission accomplished at last. But we could not be absolutely certain this was the exact place.

"But I'm close!" I whispered fiercely. "I may be off by a mile or two, *but I'm close!"*

Later, as our now-exhausted group climbed aboard an El Al 761 for the flight home, I was hit with a thrilling parallel.

Friend, we don't know when Jesus will come. And the recent, tragic debacle over "88 Reasons Why the Rapture Will Occur in '88" is just one more pointless squabble in man's never-ending effort to discount the Bible warning: "No man knows the day or the hour."

It may be six months. It may be six years. It may even be 60 years. I don't know when, and neither do you.

But we're close! We can know that for sure.

For any one of us, it's only a short lifetime away.

My older brother Dan—yes, he's a pastor too—recently conducted a funeral service for an elderly saint named Ethel. He told the sober congregation how he had spent some time with her just hours before she passed away.

Both of them knew the end was very, very near as they talked quietly together. Ethel was in some pain, but spiritually composed and almost good-humored about her situation.

As their visit drew to a close, Dan pulled his chair nearer and gently asked, "How do you feel about what lies ahead for you?"

A soft smile crossed Ethel's face. "Heaven is very near," she murmured. Indeed, for her it was only hours away. She could almost reach out and touch the face of God Himself.

And those of us sitting there reflecting during that memorial service felt much the same way. It's so near! So real and so near.

As you read these pages, may it grow to be real and near for you as well.

God bless you on your journey home.

Cheerios and Streets of Gold

--------------------- 1 ---------------------

When I get to heaven, gonna put on my shoes, gonna walk all over God's heaven."

Is *that* why you want to go?

How about this one that my daughter Karli sang when she was 6 years old? "I will wear a crown in my Father's house."

There are many good reasons to look forward to heaven. I have a list, and I'm sure you do too. Some of my reasons are simple and surface; others are so intensely personal and precious that I don't even whisper them to my wife.

Reasons to look forward to going home.

* * *

Whenever I think about heaven and my reasons for wanting to go there, I remember a little boy coming to America. My parents were missionaries. As early as I can remember, we lived in Thailand. I was 6 years old when we began planning our first furlough to our home in the United States.

As the special day approached, I experienced several very interesting emotions. What does it feel like to go home to a country that has never been your home? What does a 6-year-old kid know about citizenship?

I began'to feel American on several levels. During that furlough, and especially on subsequent furloughs as I had more memories and attachments to recall, I began to feel increasing loyalty based on several different values. The first level was simple. I had a love for America based—and I'll be frank—on its physical features, its physical delights. America was a land that had big air-conditioned cars with power windows. Beautiful eight-lane freeways. To a little boy who was used to beat-up Volkswagen buses and dusty 300-mile trips on dirt roads, even America's freeway system was a great reason for national pride.

Then there were supermarkets. All those shelves loaded with everything we couldn't get overseas! Milk in cartons— *regular* milk that didn't start out as powder and clump in the bottom of the glass. Strawberries. Apples. Pears. Cheerios. I could tell you stories about Cheerios. My grandparents are still in debt from buying Cheerios for four little boys.

And there was so much more. Television. Disneyland. Escalators. We rode up and down escalators until the security guards came for us. Yes, we loved America, all right. America the Beautiful—Land of Plenty.

A trip home to America also meant a return to people like us. In the mission field we were oddities. We were different. Especially in the little villages, I remember little old ladies coming up to rub our cheeks, to feel our pale skin. Furlough meant at least temporary escape from that. In America we fit in; we spoke the same language. It felt good to belong.

And then there was citizenship.

* * *

As I grew older, I came to appreciate that America is more than just creature comforts and English-speaking grocery checkers. Those patriots at the Battle of Lexington didn't fight and die just so I could enjoy freeways and trips to Magic Mountain. Every time I returned home to the U.S., I had an increased appreciation for the fact that I was a citizen. And something about that citizenship drew me toward home.

Even as a little toddler in a foreign land, I was still an American citizen. The whole heritage of the United States of America belonged to me.

Everywhere I traveled, I had the rights and privileges of a U.S. citizen. A passport with my picture on it gave me rights—inalienable rights. The U.S. government paid for a consulate and an ambassador just to look after my needs as an American. The U.S. Army had orders to make sure I was always safe.

Until you live overseas, it's not possible to truly understand what it feels like to look out of a plane window and see on the horizon the California coastline, American soil, and know that down there is the country you belong to. Citizenship is a wonderful blessing.

But there's something that goes even beyond a loyalty based on citizenship. A love for your country based on your growing conviction in the rightness of its foundations.

I love my country today because of my belief in the rightness and the goodness of its ideals. I say that with my eyes wide open. Even with slums and Iran/contra and televangelists' scandals and the S&L mess and crime and pornography and drug abuse, there's still a rightness about America that gives me a fierce loyalty.

Love for my country springs from a conviction that democracy is right and totalitarianism is wrong. Freedom of speech is right; censorship is wrong. Religious freedom is right and state-run churches are wrong. I love America because it epitomizes the best of so many noble ideals.

But what about heaven? As soon-to-be citizens of that fair land, can the same motivations apply?

* * *

Remember the Cheerios and the eight-lane freeways? In heaven there are streets of gold. Fruit from the tree of life. Flowers that never fade.

And mansions. "I go to prepare a place for you," Jesus promised. And what a place! God tells me I simply can't imagine it all. "Eye hath not seen . . . " Remember? Still, it's good to try. Clear rivers. A city adorned as a bride. No more tears. It's a long, wonderful list held out for our inspection by a loving Father who can't wait for homecoming day.

How about being with people who are like you? People with a common purpose, a common bond? Millions of heavenly citizens who enjoy a common denominator—an overwhelming gratitude to Jesus for the gift of salvation?

I'm acquainted with many, many Christians who are

15

different from me in many ways. Different races. Different political viewpoints. Different family loyalties. Different doctrinal views. Love for differently uniformed NBA basketball teams I do not particularly care for. But we enjoy a common bond in Christ. In heaven we will be surrounded by people who think as we do on that one great issue.

There will never be arguments in heaven. There won't be misunderstandings or feuds or rifts. Not one. In heaven we'll enjoy a furlough from fighting.

Then there's citizenship. What a feeling to realize that by the grace of God I am a citizen of heaven! I've accepted God's rulership in my life; that makes me a citizen of heaven. I *belong* there. Heaven is my home.

As citizens of heaven we have become heirs to all the rights and privileges that go with citizenship. All of heaven's protection, all of heaven's infinite spiritual resources, all of heaven's interest in our needs, is ours. We are enfranchised members.

Finally, my loyalty to heaven is based on the rightness of its cause. Just as I believe in democracy and the free enterprise system, I believe with all my heart in the rightness of the government of heaven, in the broad principles that God has ordained to run His universe.

Mark it down: God's government is right and Satan's is wrong. God is fair and Satan isn't. God is truthful; Satan's not. God is holy and good and loving, while the enemy is none of these.

Wouldn't you like to live eternally where things are done right? It makes you eager to go there right now, doesn't it? "Even so, come, Lord Jesus."

But, you know, I neglected to tell you the number one reason why a blond-haired little boy looked forward to going home. People I loved lived there!

* * *

Grandma and Grandpa lived in America. Going home meant going to be with them. It meant a grand reunion with

16

hugs and kisses and tears of joy. A delicious feeling of *completeness* on the ride home from Los Angeles International Airport.

No more getting by on airmail letters. No more reel-to-reel tape recordings, filled with off-key trumpet solos and awkward greetings. We were home! Face-to-face with those we loved the most!

When I look forward to heaven, I believe the same thing is true. Golden streets are nice. Fresh fruit and mansions are nice. Worshiping with fellow believers will be nice. Citizenship in heaven and an appreciation for the righteous government of God are wonderful.

But how about that reunion with Jesus? How about the experience of looking on His face? Seeing those nail prints? Walking and talking with Him?

Let's never forget it—Jesus is the best part of heaven. Without Him there, heaven would ultimately be a very luxurious vacation, but endlessly dull. We'd soon be tired of it if Jesus weren't there.

Jesus is the author of our heavenly citizenship. He's the reason for it. He's the Creator of it. And He's the central reason why citizenship—heavenly citizenship—is a priceless possession.

"Gonna see my friend Jesus, down by the riverside." Now *that's* one worth singing.

Surprised by Joy

2

S urprise!"
The lights suddenly come on throughout the house. Noisemakers blare. Fifty leering faces pop out of your broom closets and from behind the living room sofa.

Don't you just love it?

Perhaps you're the type who pastes on a happy smile for the duration of the evening, then mutters to your wife as the last guest leaves, "Don't you ever do this to me again! I told you I hate surprises."

I must confess that just once I was *had*—and good. I was working the graveyard shift as the switchboard operator at a large hospital near the college I attended.

Already bleary-eyed from a long, napless day of classes, I clocked in and reluctantly prepared to begin eight interminable hours staring at rows of phone circuits. At least I had one activity already picked out: I was determined to feel sorry for myself all night, because I had to work on my birthday.

Suddenly, there stood my girlfriend with three of my best buddies carrying cake, ice cream, paper plates, root beer—the works! At midnight! What a surprise! I almost punched the code blue button by mistake. That was one party I will never forget!

Can you recall a moment when you knew a surprise—a *good* surprise—was coming your way, but you didn't know the details yet? What a delicious moment.

"Mr. Smith, this is Ed McMahon calling from Publisher's Clearinghouse Sweepstakes—"

A letter from a major publishing company: "Your manuscript just arrived, and guess what!"

"This is the Pontiac dealer down on Elm. Your friend was in here yesterday filling out a door prize card for our new sport model Grand Am in your name. Well, hold on to your hat!"

Never mind the details—something tells me it's going to be a good day!

* * *

Surprised by joy. Forgive me for borrowing that classic C. S. Lewis title, but it expresses so well the poignant moment when a person senses impending good news.

My heart is touched when I read a Bible story in which someone was surprised by joy. Imagine the day when the aging Jacob looked down the road to see his sons, breathless and dusty, rushing to blurt out unbelievable news. "Joseph is alive!"

Can you picture that first emotion-laden moment of confusion? "What? How can—?"

I don't know the Hebrew equivalent for "Are you kidding?" but Jacob must have repeated it over and over until that magnificent headline finally sank in.

How about that Sunday morning in Jerusalem when 11 devastated disciples tried to pick up their shattered lives. Their hopes and dreams crushed by Friday's Calvary, they, along with Lazarus, the Marys, Jesus' mother, and others, try to comfort one another in the morning's numbing silence.

And then the news begins to rumble through town. "Jesus has risen from the grave!"

Visualize that first moment when Peter takes hold of the truth. Or John. Or Mary, the mother of Jesus. "He's alive!" What a tremendous moment!

There's a day coming when billions of God's children will be surprised by joy. One way or another, I have every intention of being there to see it happen.

It's going to take place on resurrection day at the Second Coming.

Many of God's faithful have been laid to rest. They're sleeping quietly in their graves waiting for the wake-up call of the returning Life-giver.

I've been to memorial services when the pastor gently described the peaceful, dreamless rest of God's saints. De-

19

cades, even centuries, pass by as a moment, the "twinkling of an eye"; the turmoil and hatred and conflict of these last days are unknown to the dead who are sleeping in Christ. So much in Scripture corroborates this vital truth that the dead are simply unconscious in the grave.

Until . . . the day.

First Thessalonians 4 describes the beautiful morning when the trumpet will sound "and the dead in Christ shall rise."

Oh, how my departed loved ones, my close friends who have been laid to rest, will be surprised by joy that day! That wonderful moment of divinely ordained confusion!

* * *

I have a shame-faced recollection dating back to my early teen years when I was attending a boarding school in Singapore. On lazy weekend afternoons—and you may find this difficult to understand—guys would pass the time of day in a way only bored teens can appreciate.

It had been discovered that if you took three or four deep breaths and then had one of the sturdier students squeeze you around the chest from behind, you would momentarily faint. Actually pass out. Weird.

I guess we were just hard up for entertainment, but I remember the great hilarity that ensued from watching someone black out for those few seconds and then slowly come to, a look of brief confusion on his face before the full state of consciousness returned.

I heard later some malicious rumor that you actually end up lowering your IQ by two or three points every time you try this stunt. Thank goodness I did it only 20 or 30 times. To this day, I feel fine, except that I can't spel so good. But I will not forget that very momentary sense of confusion, and the spiritual lesson it has always held for me.

* * *

I have a favorite grandfather—"Grandpa Venden"—who passed away in 1973. My family was serving in the mission field. Helplessly stuck overseas as I was during that painful time, I couldn't attend his funeral. All I have are memories.

And what memories. His personality, his inimitable wit, his bigger-than-life preacher's grin, his overwhelming love for his Jesus.

He had 11 grandkids who loved him for his jokes, his scribbled notes on birthday cards, his softball pitching (always delivered in dress pants with necktie still intact), his twinkling eye.

But he was laid to rest. His final memories were in a hospital bed, his body racked with the pain of cancer.

I wasn't there for those last moments. But there had to be that one *final* moment, the last glimpse of life, the last slender shred of consciousness.

And then the welcome darkness of sleep.

Many years have passed since then. Grandkids have grown up, jobs have come and gone, four new U.S. presidents have served—all without his knowledge. He's resting.

But the trumpet will sound. From a quiet gravesite in St. Helena, California, Grandpa Venden will be called forth to new life.

There will be one noble moment, one flickering moment, of delicious confusion—that moment of conscious transfer from the pain and stark whiteness of the hospital bed to this wonderfully baffling new moment of resurrection. The trumpets. The choirs of angels. The King on His cloud looking, I'm sure, right into my grandpa's eyes. "Come forth, Dan!"

For just a moment . . . "What? What? Where did—? Where am I? The hospital—?"

Then, with a mighty rush of understanding, Grandpa Venden, who for some 50 years preached the resurrection truth, will realize what has happened. It will hit him all at once: "It was all true!"

I will let you in on a secret. When that moment of delicious confusion takes place, it will partly be because my Grandpa Venden is also going to be looking into the grinning faces of three daughters, 11 grandchildren, assorted children-in-law, and, at last count, 22 great-grandkids from the generation he never knew, all post-1973.

As far as I know, every last one of the tribe is pledged to be there that day just to see the look on his face.

But he always was a sharp old guy. I expect that look of confusion to last but a moment. I can hear him already: "Hey, get me out of here! What have I missed?"

Within 10 minutes he'll know all the great-grandkids' names, have three of them on his lap, and be bragging to them all about the 22 youngsters who had the most wonderful great-grandpa there ever was.

There's a TV commercial for some local sales event that ends with the sincere warning: "Don't you dare miss it!" When I think of that upcoming moment of treasured reunion in the church cemetery, I take that warning to heart. I have no intention of missing it. Count on me to be there.

* * *

And now some more moments of being surprised by joy.

I don't know many details about the trip to heaven. But I do know that we can anticipate an overwhelming rush of emotion as the reality slowly and deliciously sets in. "This is real! We waited, we believed, we hoped . . . but we never quite grasped it. It's real!"

Sometime during the trip I expect that many of us will quietly murmur, "It's really happening. This is no dream."

Surprised by joy.

I have a favorite passage found in Psalm 24 that goes like this: "Lift up your heads, O ye gates; and be ye lift up, ye everlasting doors; and the King of glory shall come in." Then comes the question: "Who is this King of glory?" And the answer: "The Lord strong and mighty, the Lord mighty in battle."

Maybe you've sung that chorus, as I have many times. It's one of the highlights from Handel's *Messiah*. Always it has sounded so grand and glorious to me, though I realize it must be just a pale copy of the original.

My friend, as we approach heaven's gates, *we will hear that song.* For real.

Will the tune be the same? Maybe. Heaven's choirs, with a twinkle in their collective eyes, may sing it the way we've learned it down here, just for fun. You know, so we can hum along.

But imagine the sensation when, listening to that song sung by the group it was originally composed for, we discover that Jesus, King of kings and Lord of lords, the One whom the song was originally written to honor, is right there present with us. We will say it—we will say it again and again, with reverence and tears in our eyes and overflowing gratitude in our hearts, "My God, thank You that we are here, really, truly here. We can hardly believe it's real!"

Surprised by joy. Don't you dare miss it.

My Father, the President

3

I am 34 years old as I write this chapter. It's just three days since my family and I finished celebrating my birthday.

I don't imagine you're interested much, but I share this to lead to some bad news. I am beginning to pick up just a sense, as the years go by, that one of my all-time fantasies is never going to happen.

I shall never play right field for the Los Angeles Dodgers.

I realize this now. I don't feel that old, but I'm startled to discover that practically every Dodger on the 1989 roster is younger than I am except for Lasorda. I'm older than Kirk Gibson, if you can imagine that, and everyone knows how hobbled up he is.

For years I have fantasized about catching fly balls—extremely routine fly balls, by the way—and gunning them on nine hops into second base. Taking mighty swings at fastballs (my fantasy swings are really not too bad) and rocketing pitch after pitch deep into the left field pavilion.

But now, at age 34, I face the truth: there's no way. I can call the Dodgers, but they're not going to call me.

Another dream that is fading fast is the one in which I will someday be able to slam-dunk in basketball.

It's so unfair! I'm over six feet two, reasonably fit, with all the desire in the world. But even on a good day, when I can leap mightily, I barely scrape the bottom of the rim with my longest fingernail.

Slam-dunk with authority? No way. Not without a chair to stand on.

Every now and then, at midnight when the moon is full, I have a dream in which I can really do it. I dribble the ball toward the hoop, gather my strength, take off . . . and soar higher and higher, all in slow motion, and *mash* that basketball home!

It's a great dream. Over and over I slam the ball through the hoop, scarcely able to believe I've mastered it at last!

In my dream my three brothers and dad, all shorter than I, are standing around shaking their heads in jealous disbelief. "How do you *do* that?"

"It's so easy." I shrug with just the right touch of nonchalance. "Here, let me do another one for you." Boom!

What a painful moment when I awake with a start and realize that I'm still attached to the same weak, land-based legs I crawled into bed with.

While we're on this maudlin topic, I may as well confess my fear that I will never be invited to direct a 350-voice choir in Handel's *Messiah,* accompanied by full orchestra. The years just roll by while I make zero progress toward this long-cherished objective. I have my tuxedo ready, I've got a copy of the music, but the phone never rings.

One cherished dream has by now faded clear off the radar screen. I always wanted my dad to be president.

* * *

What a life! The son of the president of the United States. Steven Ford, Chip Carter, Ron Reagan, and now several hundred Bush kids. But not me.

Reality lands with a thud. When your dad is 60 years old, working as a pastor in a medium-sized church, and hasn't made even his first move toward the White House, you can forget it.

(On the other hand, now that I think about it, with fellow ministers Pat Robertson and Jesse Jackson running every four years, maybe Dad is on his way! Stay tuned.)

Try to imagine all the perks of having your dad as president . . .

"We're off to the Soviet Union for the summit trip. Why don't you come along, son? . . . Don't worry about that; the State Department can rustle you up a passport. . . . I'll send an Army transport plane to pick you up."

Or: "Why don't you drop by for supper tonight? Maybe we

can go swimming in the White House pool afterward. . . . Sure, bring her along. The limo will be over about 7:00. By the way, I've invited Magic Johnson too."

Just think of it all. Restful weekends in the rustic elegance of Camp David. Suppers on the presidential yacht cruising the Potomac. Lively arguments with Sam Donaldson. Decent seats at Redskins games.

And of course, no more job worries. Someone will always be happy to sign me on as an international consultant or pay me to host a TV show.

But better than all the physical comforts and unique travel opportunities would be the knowledge that the president of the United States cared about *me!* Night after night I could put my head down on my pillow and drift into peaceful sleep, knowing that Dad was in the White House looking after my interests.

It's a wonderful thing indeed to have powerful friends in high places. And to have your dad be the president would be just about the best security there is.

No legislation would be introduced that was detrimental to your interests. In weighing policy decisions, the president would thoughtfully muse to himself, "How will this impact my son?" Not bad.

I read once that many years ago two small boys made themselves entirely too much at home in the White House. They slid down banisters, they ran noisily up and down the hallways, they even—horrors!—poked their heads into a crowded cabinet meeting.

But their last name was Lincoln. So, needless to say, they got away with it all. It's nice when Dad is president.

* * *

My favorite Lincoln story is of the distressed mother who went to see the president about her son, who was sentenced to die for sleeping on guard duty for the Union army. President Lincoln, who had developed quite a reputation for pardoning such soldiers, scrawled on a piece of paper that the private was not to be shot "until further orders from me. Signed, A. Lincoln."

The mother, her worries still intact, wondered aloud to the president when those orders would be issued. With a slow smile, he drawled, "Ma'am, if your son lives until those further orders arrive, he will live to be a good deal older than Methuselah."

Yes, it is good to have the president on your side! For most of us, this will be a dream unfulfilled. But would you settle for the King of the universe?

* * *

My Father, the King. Not of Siam, the country of my childhood. Not king of some small, obscure Middle Eastern kingdom of the mythical variety always featured on *Mission: Impossible.* But King of the universe.

And He is on my side. Try as I may, it just doesn't sink in easily.

I have had a dad and I am a dad. And every now and then I am able to grasp just a tiny piece of the puzzle that is God the Father/King.

I watched my little daughter emerge into this world. What an emotion-laden moment! And God has felt that.

I felt her tiny arms cling to me when the neighbor's dog growled menacingly. She needed me in her moment of 2-year-old's terror. God has felt that too.

I've felt her warm, wet kiss on my cheek as she says a bashful "Thank you, Daddy" after opening a Christmas present. And God has even felt that.

I have felt strong, protective, filled with righteous assertion as I have paraded next door to protect her from bullies or into the principal's office to defend her against her accusers.

And so does God. He is on our side like a perfect dad. I can say this without any false pride: I would die for my girls. Willingly, unhesitatingly. And God . . . Need I say more?

And what are the ramifications of having a perfect and all-powerful Father as King?

27

I remember an amusing series of TV commercials a number of years ago. They always involved some poor soul who was stuck on a desert island or on a raft in the lonely Pacific. Sharks would begin to circle around, enemy gunboats appear on the horizon.

Somehow there was always a telephone handy. (The beauty of television.) One quick call, and dozens of Navy troops would magically appear to rescue the hapless drifter from the jaws of death. Then on the screen the words "Aames Home Loans to the rescue!"

God is prepared. The King has an army ready to defend. The angel hosts are on call 24 hours a day. Whether I need physical safekeeping or moral protection, His troops will be sent upon request.

* * *

How else is our King's support felt?

In this day of "name it and claim it" and prosperity gospels, I can at least find courage in the Bible's simple promise: "Thy bread and water shall be sure."

It doesn't appear to be God's will that I ever get rich, and I can live with that. But it's good to know that He is interested in keeping me fed.

There hasn't been a change in administration since the Israelites ate manna three times daily. Or since ravens made food deliveries to the prophet Elijah down by Cherith Brook. Or since God Himself, with a small smile playing about His lips, distributed five loaves and two small fish among more than 5,000 goggle-eyed listeners after an all-day meeting.

He's the same God still, with the same abilities and loving instincts He always had.

Money? Again, God hasn't chosen to give me very much of it. But if His followers can pull coins out of a random fish's mouth, I guess I don't need to worry much about money.

One of my uncle's favorite sermon illustrations is of the man who was beset with financial worries but then hired someone to do all his worrying for him. He was bragging to a friend about this new "Worry Services, Inc."

"How much does it cost you?" the acquaintance wanted to know.

"Four hundred bucks a month."

"Four hundred a month! You haven't got that kind of money. How in the world are you going to pay him?"

"That's the first thing he has to worry about!"

And we *can* let God do the worrying!

* * *

I had lunch with a Christian businessman the other day. He confided to me that he was very wealthy. "My dad is rich," he intimated quietly.

"Is that right? What kind of business is he in?"

"Oh, he's in the cattle business."

"Where is his ranch?" I tried to sound interested.

The man took a bite of muffin, then went on as if he hadn't heard. "Yeah, he's very rich. He owns all the cattle on a thousand hills."

Silence. "Oh. You mean *Him.*"

But when I thought about it later, that little exchange grew in significance. My Father is "rich in houses and lands," as the old hymn says. Heaven's resources, heaven's treasure houses are at my disposal. Some now, and plenty down the road a bit.

Well, money and power and helicopter rides to Camp David are fine. But have you noticed the greatest truth of all? Presidents seem to go on loving their children even when they make mistakes. Do I need to list examples for you? Just think back over the past 20 years or so, and plenty of headline stories will come to mind without my listing them here. Presidents love their wayward children, and that's all there is to it.

And our Father up in heaven, in His wisdom, gave us 66 books filled with the mistakes and flubs and outright crimes of some of His favorite people. A sordid record indeed—and one that speaks volumes to His sin-prone children living today.

Abraham was a liar. David an adulterer and murderer.

Noah a drunk. Peter was a chickenhearted bigmouth. Elijah a fleet-footed coward. Solomon a womanizer who puts any of today's candidates to shame.

And God loved them all. He was on their side, gently drawing them to Himself. Forgiving, reforming, always loving and accepting.

God loves sinners. What transforming power that knowledge brings! How it changes lives! And prayers! And relationships!

* * *

I remember an incident years ago when my older daughter was just a skinny kid in third grade or so. She had been naughty, and I had been called to school. I remember her look of terror as I came into the administration building.

I will never forget her relief as I calmly took care of things and drove her home. Later we had a quiet conversation.

"I want you to know," I told her, "that you can always call me if you are in trouble. I will come and help you anytime, anywhere.

"If you're in trouble at school, you can call and I will come. If the neighbor kids are beating up on you, I will take care of it. If you're down at the police station and they want to lock you up, you can call and I will come. If you're in trouble with some boy and don't know where to turn, you can come to me and I will help you.

"There is nothing you can do that will ever keep me from loving and defending you. Nothing."

Things have been different between me and God since then. I believe God can be trusted with knowledge of our frailties. Our prayers can be brutally frank as we tell Him in no uncertain terms where we're messing everything up. It's not going to matter; His love will still shine forth in its full strength.

What a God! My Father, the King!

And what about heaven?

* * *

Our Father, the King, has gone to prepare a place for us. John 14:1-3 is a potent promise to every child of the King. At this very moment the heavenly White House is being prepared for its guests. Soon, very soon, we will dwell with our God, the King.

All the privileges, all the perks, all the little niceties that make being related to royalty such a delight will be ours. Best of all, we will sit down at the supper table night after night and dine in fellowship with the King Himself.

It's great to be related to Someone like that.

A Ride Through Time

―――――――――――――――― 4 ――――――――――――――――

I confess I am fascinated by TV's time machines. You know, those fantastic devices that take a person back in history to see firsthand how things used to be; or forward, to see the shape of things to come. The notion has been around for ages. H. G. Wells titled a book *The Time Machine* back in 1890. Most sensible people scoffed.

But I understand that Einstein changed that. According to his theories, traveling back through time is *possible*—though it's not likely ever to happen. Which is probably just as well, because so many people would want to travel to the past when their health was better and their friends were closer and burritos at Taco Bell were only 25 cents, that there might not be anyone left to live here in the present. Just about the only way to indulge this kind of fantasy is through the imaginary miracles of Hollywood.

There are several kinds of these films around. You may have seen one or two on TV. There's the "machine" picture, in which somebody travels into the future in some gizmo like the famous DeLorean. There's the "time warp" movie, too. But let's not forget the simplest variety of all, in which someone simply wishes himself into the past to meet some cute girl of a bygone era.

These films always gloss over a number of glaring inconsistencies. The theory always exists that tomorrow and yesterday are both happening today, *somewhere,* and that somehow we can figure out how to get there from here.

One always unaddressed, and therefore never answered, question is: If I travel to tomorrow, will there be a me already there? And what about the past? Are there two of me now, or three? If there's another me (or two more of me), can I borrow money from . . . him/them? Baffling questions. Don't ask. Enjoy.

In my weaker moments of greed, I try to imagine the living I could make traveling forward 10 or 20 years and coming back and predicting all the World Series games or gaining national respect as a master political pundit. (Who but me would ever predict the McGovern-Eagleton ticket? or that Bush would pick Quayle?)

It's easy to get carried away having fun like this. And yet—

I have at times sensed a hint of spiritual truth in this fascinating concept of time travel. I get a glimpse of a God who knows the future and yet is not bound by it. A God who can paint for us, through His biblical prophets, panoramic pictures—with eyewitness accuracy—of tomorrow's events.

* * *

One film in particular gave me a unique challenge. It was a simple story, really. Boy falls in love with photo of girl; boy travels back in time to meet girl; boy falls in love with actual girl; boy gets suddenly yanked back to the present; boy, lonely for girl, dies of a broken heart; film ends.

Well, there was more. But the crux of the story was that when this successful playwright, who had everything going for him, is violently wrenched back to the 1970s, he discovers that all the pleasant trappings of his era—his condo, car, color TV—hold no meaning for him anymore. His every thought and desire are to return to the woman he loves.

It was pretty soapy stuff. But it made me think about heaven.

Heaven beckons invitingly to the Christian, yet it lies in the future. And the future is maddeningly inaccessible. There's no way to get there except wait. Work and wait.

In another film, the chief character, impersonating H. G. Wells, is asked which direction he will travel in his new time machine, past or future.

"Future," he responds without a moment's hesitation, "because I belong there."

My guess is that if they had a similar chance, most Christians would say the same. They'd climb in, buckle up,

H-3

and eagerly zoom forward to the very day when Jesus Christ returns and eternal life with Him begins. The best shortcut ever taken.

But there's no such machine.

And so we work and wait.

My sobering question is this: WHAT IF we could somehow travel to heaven—even for just 24 hours?

Twenty-four hours in heaven . . . then back to live out our days here. What impact would that brief trip have? How would we then live?

"Faithful men of old" made the journey. Prophets of God in Bible times, through the divine gift of vision, saw that fair land just as vividly as if they'd had a free ride to the pearly gates.

Isaiah traveled to a Paradise full of gardens and vineyards, where wolves and lambs live in peace, where little children lead docile lions in grassy meadows.

John describes heaven beautifully in the final chapters of Revelation: the river of life, the magnificent throne of God, the leaves of the tree "for the healing of the nations." He tells us he saw a loving Saviour wiping away tears.

Yes, Virginia, time travel *is* possible. It is a rare gift of God to His faithful messengers. Their brief journeys to heaven give us courage to wait. Eagerly.

* * *

There was one frequent time traveler that to this day few are aware of.

Ellen Harmon was a teenage girl living in Maine in the middle 1800s. Frail but deeply religious, she was part of the Millerite movement that swept the nation's major denominations. She survived the Great Disappointment when Christ did not return to earth in 1844 as so many expected.

In her mid-teens, Ellen began to have dreams. Or visions, if you like. Vivid experiences that were clearly supernatural.

In several of them, she said, the beauty of heaven was unfolded to her. Her published experiences, read by many

34

thousands of Christians ever since, contain descriptions that read like eyewitness accounts.

For some 70 years this humble Christian woman, who later wrote under her married name of White, produced some of the most powerful Christian books I have ever read. Her writing was largely responsible for the birth of one of today's fastest-growing Christian denominations, the Seventh-day Adventist Church.

Two special favorites, *The Desire of Ages* and *Steps to Christ,* have been as helpful as any books I can recommend to anyone who wants to become acquainted with our Lord. Whatever your church background, I invite you to try them.

Some have hailed her dreams as prophetic.

Others label her a fraud. Still others simply read and are wonderfully blessed. You can debate if you want to about the validity of such visions. Their legitimacy, however, is not the point I want to make.

The lesson I invite you to consider is this: Young Ellen *saw,* or believed she saw, the glory of heaven. She was there. She described, as best human language can, what the land God is preparing for us is really like.

What is more, she looked upon the face of Jesus. She listened as He spoke words of comfort and encouragement to her. That voice—she never forgot it.

But then the vision would end. The light of Paradise would fade. The image and unforgettable voice of Christ would slowly disappear. And the dark reality of nineteenth-century New England would abruptly return.

She tried to describe the devastation of that return. "So dark," she would murmur. "Oh," she sighed with the psalmist, "that I had wings like a dove, then would I fly away and be at rest." It's painful to time-travel to heaven and then have to take the reluctant return trip back home.

But how did she then live? How did that brief trip change her life?

* * *

In a lifetime that spanned nearly nine decades and produced scores of best-selling major books and articles, Ellen Harmon lived for one thing: a reunion with her Saviour. She lived it, breathed it, witnessed about it, wrote about it: Jesus . . . Jesus . . . Jesus. Oh, to be with Him.

She poured her life into service for her Saviour.

She and her husband, James, literally gave their existences to the cause of Christ. Her life of service on three continents has been hailed by religious leaders of many denominations as a milestone of humble achievement.

One day in heaven. One look at the face of Jesus. And nothing is ever the same again.

How would *we* then live?

* * *

I find it is well worth the time spent wrestling with that question. How would 24 hours in heaven with my Saviour change my life?

Would my devotional life change? Would the words in my Bible come alive with new meaning? Would my prayers to a now-tangible Friend be transformed?

Would I be more faithful in taking that necessary time each day? Perhaps I would learn to think of that quiet time as more of an appointment or glad reunion than as a duty.

Would my participation in church with the body of Christ be any different? That's an interesting question to consider. Would our testimony to our brothers and sisters in the Lord have new meaning? I rather think so.

Is it possible that my lifestyle would change as well? My leisure time activities? The things I read, watch, and listen to? Having traveled heaven's avenues, would I now understand better what kinds of things belong . . . or don't belong?

I have even considered that one trip to heaven might change what I put in the offering plate each weekend. Financial priorities might be drastically altered, perhaps permanently, by that one glimpse.

The list continues . . . but that's *my* list. Perhaps you need one as well.

Millions of lives have been changed as people, in their own simple way, have somehow caught a glimpse, one small impression of a waiting heavenly home and the waiting, saving Jesus.

Millions have lived for the return journey, been martyred for it, given their all for it. They will not be disappointed.

Take the trip.

And be forever changed.

One Mile From the Pearly Gate

5

The electric chair.

The gas chamber.

Horrifying words, aren't they? They shove into our national consciousness the ugliest side of the American scene.

Our nation was stretched nearly to its emotional limit recently over the execution of a fresh-faced young man named Ted Bundy. Talk about an emotional teeter-totter for the country!

You read the hard-to-believe stories, I'm sure. Hooting, jeering crowds outside the Florida penitentiary lighting sparklers and throwing rocks at the hearse as it left the parking lot afterward. Crude signs: "Thank God It's Fryday!" Gruesome rumors: a local fast-food restaurant was alleged to be selling "Bundy fries" to grinning patrons, along with its regular burgers and milk shakes.

One local radio station, I understand, on the morning a condemned man goes to the electric chair, has a regular routine. It broadcasts the sound of a steak sizzling on the stove while the DJ chortles, "This is for you, scum!"

Meanwhile, one heartbroken mother remembers an innocent little baby born through her tears and pain and hope. Quietly she weeps for all the victims and wasted deaths, including the one taking place that day.

Yet out of the numbing hopelessness of capital punishment comes a dramatic story that brings us close to heaven.

But first, join me for a brief trip to San Quentin's death row.

* * *

You are there waiting for your execution in this dreary prison's gas chamber. Every legal appeal has been exhausted; every probable and improbable escape avenue has been explored. Unless the world comes to an end first, you will meet your fate in that little room downstairs.

What is more, you are doomed to face death with no knowledge of a Saviour or any hope of a resurrection. You do not believe, you never have, and you're not about to start now. One way or another, you're going to get through this on your own, thank you. The date approaches and increasingly crowds your consciousness. It gets more and more difficult to find distractions, to get any sleep. That room downstairs looms larger and larger.

I've heard that years ago the inmates on death row in a certain prison had access to one old black-and-white TV set. It was always placed in front of the cell of the man who was scheduled to die next.

The day comes when that infamous TV set is wheeled in front of *your* cell. Wordlessly the guard turns on the switch, adjusts the rabbit ears, and strolls away. But the stark message of that old Philco drums into your mind: YOU'RE NEXT!

Time is down to one month.

Then three weeks. Two. One.

Those last seven days slow to a trickle, then a crawl. Day and night, hour after hour, minute by dragging minute, the gas chamber waits. And remember . . . you have no Saviour, no future, no hope of anything but endless darkness.

The day before The Day arrives at last, and a small contingent of guards comes to take you downstairs to a special holding cell. There stationery is made available for last letters, final legal counsel for drawing up a will. Special meal service if you want it. Down the hall the little green room waits.

The longest night of your life passes slowly. Try as you may, you cannot keep your mind from calculating the number of hours remaining before 8:00 a.m.

Early in the morning you pick at your last meal, your hands shaking ever so slightly. Then a doctor arrives, explaining to you that he must tape a stethoscope to your chest to monitor your heart's final erratic motions.

A trio of sober-faced guards finally comes to take you to the waiting chamber. You walk down the short hallway toward the small round room with its many windows.

Already witnesses, relatives of victims, and reporters have taken their seats. Some have waited eagerly for years for this moment; others have joked and made light of the anticipated proceedings. But now nearly all of them look, well, stricken.

You are strapped into one of the two plain-looking chairs; the doctor makes one final adjustment and pats you awkwardly on the shoulder.

(The story is told that a sympathetic guard once advised a condemned prisoner, "Breathe deeply; it's easier that way." The prisoner replied with a wan smile, "How would you know?")

Everyone files out and the door clangs shut.

About that clang. Have you ever heard a prison door clang shut? There's no sound in the world like it. I used to teach a college class in a state prison. Every evening I had to pass through two sets of those doors, going in and going out. That clang still rings in my ears, the most forbidding sound I can imagine.

This door clangs shut with a finality the human mind cannot measure. You hear the big wheel on the door's outside surface being tightened, hermetically sealing the chamber to protect the innocent and kill . . . you.

Then nothing but dead silence.

You wait. Your mind, try though you will to control its final processes, darts in a million directions during these last seconds. Childhood memories of bedtime stories about Jesus. Picture-book panoramas about a place called heaven.

Is it too late? You try not to think.

Then, in the heavy silence, you hear a soft *plopping* sound beneath your chair. Small cyanide pellets have been released into a small tub of acid. Those soft, almost gentle sounds are the last you will ever hear.

About 30 seconds left. They tick by, one following another. Any breath now could be your last.

40

* * *

Welcome back to today. You're sitting comfortably in your favorite chair reading my new book. Take a deep breath before we go on.

But what we just went through together is pretty terrifying, isn't it? The mental persecution of that countdown almost qualifies as cruel and unusual punishment, if you and I would be willing to admit it.

Yet hundreds of men and women have endured it somehow, many of them with no knowledge or hope of a Saviour or life eternal. They walk into that chamber knowing and believing that life for them will end . . . and end forever that morning.

For most, it is a shattering nightmare. A babbling, shrieking, almost incoherent nightmare. A cruel death without the tiniest sliver of hope.

And then there was Sam.

* * *

Sam, like all of us, was born to a hope-filled mother. "He's such a beautiful baby," she whispered, clutching her slippery newborn to her breast as tears of pride flooded her fatigued eyes.

Her hope did not last long.

Sam was one of those characters who get off the track right from the starting gates. In and out of trouble, shiftless, never more than one step ahead of the law.

Eventually the law caught up. Sam "did time"—several times, in fact. He was a chronic small-time criminal; even while shaking hands with the warden on release day and listening impatiently to the warden's well-wishing, he would be planning his next caper.

Released from the Missouri State Penitentiary in February of 1955, Sam turned the first corner and ran smack into yet another crime adventure. A gun, an all-night restaurant, a new opportunity!

Sam prodded the lone waitress to empty the cash register into his bag, then forced her into his waiting car. Modus operandi: drive out of town a few miles and let her out. By the time she hikes home, Sam plus cash will be long gone.

All went according to the blueprint until the waitress upset the apple cart by calling him by name. "Don't think I don't recognize you, Sam," she said. "Wait till your sister gets a load of this!"

The wheels spun in his mind. *She calls the police: "Sam Tannyhill is the man you want." A positive ID. The works.*

Desperate men do desperate things. About the only thing Sam was unwilling to do was more time.

Without a word, he pulled the car off into a secluded area. A brief scuffle ensued before Sam bludgeoned the waitress to death with an automobile jack. Dumping the body, he drove on.

To make a long story short, it took police very little time to piece the whole thing together. Armed with the testimony of a taxi driver who had observed Sam's suspicious behavior at the restaurant, a great manhunt was on for Sam Tannyhill. In short order, Sam was back in jail. This time not for stealing hubcaps or old ladies' purses.

Ohio State Pen. Death row.

Time went by. The appeals process ran its course, but nobody's heart was really in it, and it was quickly apparent that Sam was going to meet his end in the state's electric chair.

Sam, who had no religious beliefs of any kind, began to prepare himself mentally to face the countdown of time.

One day he had visitors. Two men from a nearby church group came to visit. They had a reasonably amiable hour together, and when it came time to leave, one of them asked Sam if he would like to have a Bible to read. Sam startled the pair by nodding yes.

The next day one of the men returned. He had not been able to find the extra Bible he thought he had, but his little boy had offered his brand-new birthday Bible.

Sam read. And read. The men kept visiting.

Sam later described his adventures in the Word of God. "I

read where this man called Jesus turned water into wine. I decided He was a moonshiner. Then I saw where His disciples took someone's colt. I labeled Him a horse thief.

"Then I discovered that this Jesus was the Son of God and my Saviour. I began to call Him Lord."

Sam's first prayer did not ring with much spiritual maturity: "I prayed for a gun so I could shoot my way out and then go straight on the outside!" But slowly the Holy Spirit did His work with the help of His two assistants, and Sam became a changed man.

As time marched on, Elder William Fagal, a Christian minister who was also the host of the national *Faith for Today* telecast, became Sam's regular visitor. Week by week the two men enjoyed fellowship in Jesus Christ. Elder Fagal noted with amazement the spiritual growth of this new believer.

Hope began to surge within both men that perhaps Sam would not have to die after all. Sam could effectively serve the Lord in prison, witnessing and serving other inmates. So the pair reasoned. Letters from Christians began to pour into the governor's office.

Sam had asked Elder Fagal if he would be willing to be present at his execution should that date ever arrive. Inwardly trembling at the prospect, the pastor had reluctantly agreed. But several times the appointed date was postponed. Hope continued to rise.

Pastor Fagal, who lived in New York, continued to visit whenever possible, still hoping against hope that a commuted sentence might yet be arranged. One more execution date loomed larger than any had before.

The day before the execution, the minister made his customary phone call to the prison, explaining that he would fly in if necessary, but was still hoping that another postponement was in the works. The sober response came from the warden: "This time I think you had better come."

Elder Fagal arrived at the prison three hours before the appointed time of death. He was ushered into the room where Sam was eating his final meal.

"My appetite was completely taken away at the thought of

why I was there," Fagal confessed later. He did manage to pick at one small bowl of ice cream. Sam ate heartily.

What followed next was a spiritual experience that Fagal later described in a powerful little book entitled *Three Hours to Live.* He and Sam enjoyed a treasured period of closeness, Bible study, and sharing together.

"We read Bible verse after Bible verse," the pastor recalled. "Promises of the resurrection, of eternal life, of our Saviour's victory over death. One passage in particular I had planned to share, but before I could suggest it, Sam asked me to read those very verses, his favorite Bible promise: 2 Timothy 4:6-8:

" 'The time of my departure is at hand. I have fought a good fight, I have finished my course, I have kept the faith: henceforth there is laid up for me a crown of righteousness, which the Lord, the righteous judge, shall give me at that day: and not to me only, but unto all them also that love his appearing.' "

As the hour approached, Sam suggested that the two kneel in prayer. The prison chaplain and Elder Fagal both prayed, then listened as Sam poured out his heart in grateful thanksgiving to God for life and for the short months he had enjoyed as a child of God.

Elder Fagal later reconstructed the prayer as best he could. It is a touching, moving testimony.

At the end of his prayer Sam suddenly added a postscript: "And, Lord, if what these guards are about to do is a sin, please forgive them. Just charge it to my account instead."

The last precious moments trickled by. With approximately half an hour to go, prison guards came to prepare Sam for execution. A barber shaved a small area on the crown of Sam's head so an electrode could be fastened there. One trouser leg was slit up to the knee so a second electrode could be fastened just below the kneecap. Such macabre procedures, the warden explained later, often reduced a convict to jelly; Sam accepted them with utter serenity.

At the end Sam bade the warden a gracious farewell, thanking him for his many courtesies. He shook hands with the prison chaplain as well and calmly followed the guards to the plain-looking chair.

Throughout their conversation, Sam had asked Elder Fagal what time it was. Once again he did so.

"One minute to 8:00, Sam," the pastor whispered. Sam gave him a crooked grin. "Not many men know when they have just one minute of life left. I guess I'm in quite a unique position." His voice was steady.

The guards helped him into the chair and began to strap him in. Just before his arm was restrained, Sam reached out and shook Elder Fagal's hand one final time. "Goodbye, Pastor," he said, a faraway look in his eyes. *"I'll see you in the morning."*

Moments later a welder's mask was placed over Sam's face, and the warden nodded to a guard. At 8:12 p.m. the doctor made a note in his log and announced that the sentence had been carried out.

* * *

What gave Sam the inner strength to face our world's most frightening ordeal with such courage? He had his eyes on the better land.

Sam has been resting quietly in his grave for more than 30 years. Days, months, years, even decades pass by; but he is not aware of them. His last thought was of what his next thought will be: "My Lord and my King." Resurrection morning!

Electric chairs are such temporary setbacks when a man has his eyes on the better land!

* * *

Shadrach, Meshach, and Abednego faced the heat of Babylon's primitive electric chair—a fiery furnace, with the thermostat turned up 700 percent just for them.

The king was angry. Furious. Nebuchadnezzar was used to getting his own way. When he said "Bow!" most citizens got

45

down in a hurry—golden image or no golden image—and stayed down until further notice.

Now these three young followers of God stood before him.

Deep down he liked these young men. They were his top graduates; what's more, they were from the same mold as his special favorite, Daniel. There must be another way.

"Let's try this again," he suggested. "Maybe you just didn't understand the directions. We'll strike up the band once more. When you hear the national anthem on the cornet, harp, sackbut, psaltery, and dulcimer, you fellows bow down—and fast! I don't want to mention the consequences if you don't. I'll just tell you this—your God won't be much help."

Shadrach, Meshach, and Abednego faced the heathen king and his death penalty—and didn't flinch. "We don't have to carefully think of a diplomatic answer," they responded respectfully. "Our God is *able,* and He can deliver us *if He chooses to."* Then courageous words: *"But even if He does not,* we want you to know, O king, that we will not serve your gods or worship the image of gold you have set up."

Even if He doesn't. *Even if He doesn't.* Too many of us have missed this vital point. In that moment of courage, those three young men had no idea whether God would choose to save them or not. They went willingly to their place of execution with no idea what the outcome was going to be: a dramatic, divine rescue—or death.

What gave them such unflinching faith? Such courage to look Nebuchadnezzar in the face and sign their own death warrants? They had their gaze fixed on the better land.

I love the book of Daniel. Such drama! Just a few chapters after the fiery furnace, we see this same portrait of courage with Daniel in the starring role.

Daniel is the prisoner-turned-prime minister in the new Medo-Persian government. The M-P diplomats are not pleased by this elderly intruder who does his job to such perfection.

So an evil plan is put together and pitched to the gullible King Darius. And Darius, when he hears the ego-boosting pitch of his cunning advisers, begins to nod all too affably.

"Everyone is to pray only to me for 30 days? A den of lions? Not too bad, boys, not too bad. I like the sound of it. Write it up, and I'll sign it before dinner."

Too late, he realizes the trap. His hands are tied by his own foolish decree written "according to the law of the Medes and Persians, which changeth not."

Daniel, the aging prophet and loyal subject, is led to the lions' den. The shamefaced king, bitterly remorseful, assures him that his God will surely save him.

But, again, don't miss this point: Daniel entered that lions' den knowing that God was *able* to rescue, but not knowing that He *would*.

Have Christians ever been eaten by lions? You know the answer. Sometimes God shuts lions' mouths, and sometimes He doesn't. Daniel entered that dark pit of snarling beasts with nothing but a prayer and a hope.

And, friend, though the Bible does not record it, I feel safe in suggesting that Daniel entered that den with a look of calm courage. Daniel had a better night's sleep than the miserable monarch did, you can be sure of that.

Where did that courage come from? Daniel's eyes were on the better land.

Even death in a lions' den, in Daniel's mind, was but a brief interruption before his *real* life, his eternal life with God, would begin. These few short remaining years spent in an alien kingdom were nothing when the better land and the eternal kingdom of God were so near.

* * *

John Weidner, a Christian living in Paris during World War II, became an active member of a resistance team called Dutch-Paris. For several desperate years he worked day and night to help Jews and other prisoners escape from Nazi clutches. In every Gestapo headquarters, the name of Weidner was on each officer's most-wanted list.

There came a day when he and a fellow team member, Jacques Rens, were captured by the Milice police unit, which was working hand in hand with the German conquerors. Both men were tortured and beaten, but neither would give the French collaborators any information. Hoping to spark some small measure of loyalty in the French commandant, Weidner tried every means to gain his release.

One day shattering news came. Instead of the hoped-for freedom, the Vichy government had informed the Gestapo of Weidner's presence. Execution was already set for the next morning.

Now desperate, Weidner managed to persuade a sympathetic guard to help the pair escape. Following the guard's instructions to the letter, the two managed to force open the lock on their cell with some tools the guard provided. Tiptoeing past sleeping guards, the two perched themselves on an outside ledge and waited for five agonizing hours until the 6:00 a.m. curfew lifted.

You can read the dramatic story in *Flee the Captor,* by Herb Ford. I heard John Weidner tell it personally to a large audience of university students. He said, as I recall, "Those five hours were the longest of my life. I kept remembering how angels helped Peter escape from prison. But I couldn't help being reminded of John the Baptist, who lost his life in similar circumstances."

Somehow Weidner and his fellow Christian found courage to face the threat of death. They drew immeasurable strength from the knowledge that God saves some and gives the others the ability to see the better land so close on the horizon.

Just after the town clock struck 6:00, the two stretched themselves full-length from that third-story ledge and dropped to the concrete street below. Running madly for two blocks, they turned a corner and promptly slowed to a more normal pace, fighting at every step to control their urge to flee. Within a half hour the men were resting in a "safe" apartment, sharing details of their ordeal and divine escape with fellow believers.

Now living quietly in the United States, John Weidner, wearing his Medal of Freedom decoration, confesses a faith in Jesus Christ and a vision of heaven that saw him through those dark days of terror. Every border crossing, every escape from the machine guns and the torture chambers of the Nazi Gestapo, sharpened his focus on the better land.

* * *

How will it be for us? Revelation's prophecies hint of a day when God's people will face persecution from a government controlled by corrupt religious forces. Faithful believers will face death in the last days. You can count on it.

When I consider the scenarios that may yet take place, I cannot help being thankful for the great heroes of faith who direct our eyes to the better land. Shadrach, Meshach, Abednego; Daniel; Sam Tannyhill; John Weidner; and a million other courageous followers of Christ who have kept a steady gaze on heaven and the waiting home up there.

It won't be long now.

The Black-and-White Heaven

6

I'm writing this on my Apple IIe word processor on April 30, 1989. Just a few weeks ago I experienced a unique juxtapositioning of two generations that brought me up short and reminded me how far we still have to travel on our journey toward home.

I was watching a TV miniseries on the life of John F. Kennedy. Each day at lunch I would slap together a sandwich, grab an apple and a pretzel, then watch 25 minutes or so of the continuing drama that had been videotaped months before.

I was struck with the horror of the racial violence that rocked our nation in the early 1960s. I was just a boy at the time, sheltered in a faraway cocoon of Asian mission service. Now I watched.

Beatings, cross burnings, lynchings. I watched, mesmerized, as a Greyhound bus filled with freedom riders and civil rights workers was burned with the victims trapped inside. Those few who crawled out the windows were savagely beaten by angry Whites hell-bent on maintaining their unique way of life.

But the cruelest irony of this six-hour miniseries was not in the program itself, but in the commercials. Taped back in October of 1988, virtually every commercial break contained political ads for the Democratic and Republican presidential candidates in the upcoming election.

Day after day the fierce visage of Black killer Willie Horton appeared between the Kennedy scenes, and the voice-over hinted that a Dukakis presidency would release hundreds of similar madmen to rape and pillage middle America. Nearly three decades after the Kennedy dreams of equality were cut short by assassination, blatant racism was as alive as ever.

What a deadly poison it is! Scarring scenes from the

recent motion picture *Mississippi Burning* remind us of mankind's potential for hatred. Decades ago, yes, but still around us as tragically fresh as this evening's headlines.

If you have never read John Howard Griffin's shattering best-seller, *Black Like Me,* you need to. You will most likely be ashamed yet repentant as you read of our capacity to hate our brothers and sisters.

* * *

Griffin, a White novelist writing in the late 1950s, darkened his skin, then traveled the Deep South as a Black . . . in those days, a Negro. His experiences are a portrait of America's most evil tendencies toward bigotry and mindless prejudice.

Nowhere to stay. Nowhere to eat. Nowhere to sit down and rest. Nowhere even to wash up and use the restroom. Day after day the same relentless beat of mean-spirited restrictions wore down his spirit. The same "hate stare"—in the bus station, in the "Whites only" park, on the segregated city buses.

The poison of hate seemed to infect nearly everyone. A Greyhound bus driver who let Whites off the bus for restroom stops but kept the Blacks herded in the back of the bus mile after mile, hour after hour. The owner of a custard stand who sold Griffin a dish of ice cream—"We'll do business with you people," a truck driver explained—but who would not let him use a dilapidated old privy out back, telling him instead that a restroom for Blacks was "not far—thirteen, maybe fourteen blocks." Truck drivers who would pick him up, then abuse him verbally with their insatiable curiosity about the alleged sexual exploits of Black men.

Finally he found refuge with a young Black man who invited him to spend the night with his family. Out in the backwoods, in a tiny, two-room cabin, with his host's wife and six children, they ate yellow beans cooked in water and finished with tiny slices of Griffin's Milky Way bars. Then, with the smells of the swamp and the odor of urine from the zinc-bucket toilet mixing with the aroma of just-washed children, Griffin and the kids lay down on patchwork quilts and feed sacks to sleep.

But sleep did not come for Griffin as he lay there surrounded by misery. Finally he made his way outside, half-frozen, and sat alone on an overturned washtub in the foggy moonlight.

And wept. He wept with shame over the evil racism that had so divided the human family. "I thought of my daughter, Susie," he wrote afterward, "and of her fifth birthday today, the candles, the cake and party dress; and of my sons in their best suits. They slept now in clean beds in a warm house while their father, a bald-headed old Negro, sat in the swamps and wept, holding it in so he would not awaken the Negro children."

* * *

Now, some 30 years later, I still hear words that should never be used, even at the office sometimes. Harsh racial judgments uttered even at church. The venom still runs through our veins.

A Christian journalist recently wrote that racist humor seemed to be the latest trend at his children's school. Racial slurs or jokes slip out, followed by the lame amendment: "Oh, just kidding." No big deal.

Except that it is a big deal. A heaven is being prepared where racism will be forever banished. And where those who cling to its deadly vines will never be welcomed.

Back in the 1960s the brilliant humor columnist Art Buchwald wrote a bitter piece entitled "Is Heaven Segregated?" Maybe there are two heavens, he suggested, one for Whites and the other for Blacks. He went on to point out, however, that segregationists in a White heaven would have to do all their own menial work; furthermore, there would be no one there to look down on. "You can't call that much of a heaven."

He closed by observing wryly, "If there are two heavens in the hereafter, one for Whites and one for Blacks, I believe, if I were a segregationist, I'd rather go to hell."

Poignant, yes, but really not very funny. Even 25 years later, it's not very funny.

You may think to yourself, *This is for someone else.* No, it isn't. It's for you and for me. Sit quietly and ask God to remind you what your own particular brand of prejudice may be.

I remember with a shamed face flippant remarks I have made. Tiny little racial jests that formed a predictable pattern with my brothers and me. Honestly, I didn't mean a thing by them. "Some of my best friends . . ." OK. Cast the first stone if you've never done the same.

No harm done. Except it was sin.

God, convict me of my sins. Cleanse me.

The poison of prejudice takes so many subtle forms. Racial, yes. And religious. From St. Bartholomew's Massacre right down to the calculated agony of a Christian mother in 1980 Australia.

* * *

Pastor Michael Chamberlain, his wife Lindy, and their three children were vacationing at Ayers Rock in the outback down under. Their 10-week-old baby girl, Azaria—a daughter long prayed for by her devout parents—was her mother's pride. Onlookers noted Lindy's "new-mum glow" and her obvious devotion to the nursing infant.

It was the evening of August 17. Lindy had just put the baby down in the tent for the evening. She, her husband, and their two boys were chatting amiably with the other campers. Sally Lowe, a new friend, thought she heard something. So did Aidan, the Chamberlains' 6-year-old. "I think that is Bubby crying," he said.

Lindy went to check. As she approached the tent, a large wild dog, the now-famous dingo, emerged from its flap, shaking its head vigorously. In the growing dusk, Lindy could not see what, if anything, it had in its mouth.

Inside, the tent was empty. Baby Azaria had disappeared with a cry in the dark.

Thus began one of the most devastating cases of religious

bigotry in the twentieth century.

Based on *Evil Angels,* John Bryson's account of the Chamberlain murder case, 1988's Academy Award-nominated film, *A Cry in the Dark,* re-creates the public hysteria that swept the continent.

Michael and Lindy are grief-stricken but spiritually composed after the Ayers Rock ordeal. "The Bible says at the Second Coming babies will be restored to their mothers' arms," Lindy sobs to well-wishers at the campsite. "The loss of our baby is the will of God," they later explain to unsuccessful search parties and then reporters, with a calmness that irritates television audiences across Australia.

Then the rumors and gossip begin. "Did you hear the latest?" The baby's name, Azaria, supposedly meant "sacrifice in the wilderness." The Chamberlains were cult members intent on killing their own children. The family Bible had marked in red an Old Testament story about murder in a tent. There was a Jonestown connection of some sort. T-shirts proclaimed, "The dingo is innocent." And so on.

"Lies go around the world while truth is putting its boots on," a family member bitterly observes. And the flood of lies sweeps the Chamberlains into the most sensational trial in Australian history.

Did Lindy Chamberlain quietly cut her infant daughter's throat in the family car, stuff the tiny corpse into a camera bag, then cover up the deed with the help of her husband? Prosecution lawyers, despite their admission that they have no eyewitnesses, only a sketchy array of dubious scientific evidence, and not one substantiated motive for the killing, nevertheless win a conviction.

Through it all, the Chamberlains demonstrate an abiding faith in God. At one point Michael thoughtfully explains to a cynical reporter asking about their inner strength: "The Lord Jesus Christ is a very dear friend of ours, our Saviour."

Despite an outcry from Christian groups around the world, Lindy goes to prison and serves several years of a life sentence before new evidence is unearthed that results in her release. Her complete exoneration, declared publicly in September of

1988, is announced in the final credits of the film, which recently was honored with a Gold Angel by Religion in Media as best picture of the year.

Nevertheless, to this day spiritual prejudice swirls around the struggling young couple. Cries of "Baby killer!" greet Lindy when she ventures into public. Ugly strains of bigotry will likely haunt the Chamberlains until that day when they hold baby Azaria in their arms again.

* * *

Walls of hatred. Barriers. Just weeks ago I passed through the checkpoints separating West and East Germany. Long lines of motorists waited in the rain as border guards checked and double-checked and triple-checked passports and motives. Concrete walls and barbed wire and lookout towers glowered down on the grim scene.

We made it through the barrier, took a picture of the famous sign—"You are leaving the American sector"—and motored through East Germany on our way to West Berlin. Everything looked the same, yet it was easy to sense the difference.

When we passed through the second set of checkpoints after reaching the border surrounding West Berlin, I inadvertently missed a road sign. Were we in West Berlin or not? Was I in free territory?

It was a frightening sensation. Tall smokestacks and factories loomed on both sides of the road. Were they ours or theirs? I had no idea.

In a near-panic, I pulled over and stepped into a small bakery. Trying to appear calm, I approached the young lady at the counter and stammered in my rusty, college German: "Wo ist West Berlin?"

She gave me a funny look and pointed down. "Hier." Whew!

We drove around, savoring the free air, and eventually came to the famous Berlin Wall. Again we saw the familiar barbed wire, the guard towers, the foreboding spotlights. I couldn't help thinking of Reagan's challenge: "Mr. Gorbachev, tear down this wall!"

But man is seldom able to tear down the dividing walls. We can know the walls are evil, yet we seem unable to dislodge even a single brick. Century after century, they divide us from each other in countless destructive ways.

Yet walls *can* come down—as the crumbling of the infamous Berlin Wall since I wrote the opening lines of this chapter so dramatically demonstrate. Gorbachev and *perestroika* and the "influence of democracy" get the credit, but it was Someone much higher than any earthly ruler who knocked that barrier down. He had predicted it in Daniel 4:32: "The most High ruleth in the kingdom of men, and giveth it to whomsoever he will."

We read more about this barrier breaker in Ephesians 2:14: "For he [Christ] is our peace, who has made us both one, and has broken down the dividing wall of hostility" (RSV).

Jews and Gentiles. You talk about prejudice and hatred! Yet Jesus Christ tore down those walls of bigotry, bringing opportunity where there was once division. Former enemies worked side by side to spread His gospel. Persecutors became partners in the cause of Christ.

And today as well, it is only Jesus in a person's heart that causes the walls to tumble. He tears down the barriers of hostility, the barricades of prejudice.

Only Jesus . . . and ethnic enemies become workers together for God. Only Jesus . . . and former bigots learn to love and minister to homosexual AIDS victims. Only Jesus . . . and Klansmen are transformed into loving and lovable servants of the God of all mankind.

And through it all, a home is being prepared. A heavenly subdivision of homes where there will be no barriers. No red-lining of suburbs. No quotas or neighborhood watch groups seeking to maintain ethnic purity.

Think of that first day up there. That first deep breath of air that has never carried the slightest taint of prejudice. Air without the slightest toleration for hatred.

Now is the time to be getting used to that way of thinking.

Excuse Our Dust

Fraser's Hill. For hundreds of missionaries serving in the Far East, those two words are almost a synonym for heaven.

Located in the high mountains of Malaysia, Fraser's Hill is a quiet British-style vacation resort area. Large stone inns dot the mountain landscape surrounding a simple nine-hole golf course. Cool air and foggy mornings are a welcome change from the muggy tropical environment of the workaday world.

For years my family spent our annual vacation there. Following a grueling and gritty two-day train ride from Bangkok, we would endure the one-hour drive up curving mountain roads by taxi to our final destination.

Finally the cab would pull into the stone driveway at The Glen. A large, gracious inn staffed by quiet and friendly Asian personnel seemed like paradise after the arduous journey. Two unforgettable weeks in our near-heaven lay ahead.

I guess you had to be there to understand why this was such a treasured experience for battle-weary missionaries. Quietly efficient maid service. Three delicious meals provided right on schedule—hot, flaky apple pie; British steam pudding; plenty of toast with marmalade and peanut butter. Table games in the parlor every evening by the fireplace, punctuated by the servant's gentle query: "Ovaltine? Coffee?"

Comfortable, elegant service. And all of it ready and waiting when we got there.

That's a point I believe is worth making about heaven. When we get there, it will be ready and waiting for us.

* * *

When you read through the first two chapters of Genesis you discover that planning ahead is one of the divine virtues.

God got down in the dust and formed a man on the sixth day—after creating some other rather important items on days one through five.

Light on the first day. Atmosphere on the second. Dry land and a colorful blanket of vegetation to recycle that brand-new oxygen. Sunlight. I'm grateful that God creates things in just the right sequence! Vital essentials were set in place *before* oxygen-breathing, sunlight-nourished Adam was brought onto the scene.

And not just the necessities. Six full days of head-spinning creative activity filled Eden with delights. By the time God built our two wide-eyed parents, everything else was finished and tied up in a bow. "Here's your perfect world!"

How God must love getting things ready!

Have you ever had this experience on a December evening? The sun is already setting as you pull into the driveway after a hard day at work. You walk into the house and head upstairs to your bedroom, only to find the door closed. Just as you turn the doorknob, a voice from inside cries out: "Don't come in here!"

"How come?"

"I'm in here wrapping presents!"

I guess that's the one "Go away!" we never mind obeying.

In the book of John, chapter 14, Jesus makes a promise to His disciples. Remember? "I go to prepare a place for you," He pledges. You can almost hear His faint cry, can't you? "I'm up here wrapping presents!" Right now the mansions are being made ready. The streets of gold are being paved. The tree of life is watered and pruned. And the great banquet table is being set in all its white-linened elegance.

When we arrive, all will be ready for us. All of heaven's inhabitants will be standing by with broad smiles of welcome, like the staff at the world's top-rated five-star hotel. Baskets of fruit in every room and mints on every pillow.

You've seen signs in airports apologizing: "Excuse our dust. We're building for tomorrow!" It seems, in some cities at least, tomorrow never comes. Some places are perennially under construction. Cranes and barriers and detours and sandbags seem to be permanent parts of the landscape.

Not so with heaven. When we arrive, the heavenly city will be waiting in pristine perfection. Not a garish, too-much-gold, eye-blinding perfection, but a quietly gracious and unassuming top-quality kind of perfection that is oh-so-comfortable.

My Bible is bulging with evidence that ours is a God of excellence and perfection. From the daily evaluation during Creation week—"And God saw that it was good"—to His precise directions to Noah for a perfect ark to His perfect gift of a Saviour.

And during 33 short years of life on our little, mistake-laden planet, Jesus quietly demonstrated to us the excellence of heaven. In His teachings. In His sterling character. Even in His miracles.

When Jesus healed blind Bartimaeus, He didn't then hand him a pair of glasses with an apologetic disclaimer: "Here, Bart, I'm afraid you'll need these." No, it was 20-20 vision from that day on. When He healed a little crippled boy, not only did that boy throw away his crutches and corrective shoes, we can be sure he was immediately the speediest runner in the fifth-grade class.

Wondrous excellence. That's how things are done by the Personnel in heaven.

* * *

The Bible's language is too feeble—and its writers admit it—to describe the satisfying and elegant comforts of heaven. "No eye has seen, no ear has heard, no mind has conceived what God has prepared for those who love him" (1 Corinthians 2:9, NIV). Whatever we expect, heaven will be better.

Remember the old TV show *Let's Make a Deal?* Every now and then a breathless contestant would pick curtain number 3, only to see the smiling cohost reveal . . . a cage filled with 500 clucking, molting chickens. ZONK!

But then, as the sympathetic groans of the studio audience would die down, the chicken coop would be pushed aside to reveal a gleaming new sports car. Surprise! It was a good deal after all!

Let me say with all reverence, heaven will be a better deal than the best deal on *Let's Make a Deal.* Count on it. Excellence that we simply cannot imagine.

I've always wanted to visit Camp David, the presidential retreat. (I hope President Bush is reading this: I understand he devours all my books from cover to cover.) I've heard intriguing stories about its rustic elegance, its serene standards of perfection. Catered culinary delights, hand-and-foot service by military personnel, a host of leisure-time options. And all of them ready upon the president's arrival, you can be sure of that. The moment his helicopter touches down, everything is in place.

It's so easy when you're used to star treatment to forget how much effort actually goes into preparing that kind of perfection. At the television ministry where I work, we offer four quality "Partnership" weekends each year when major supporters of the ministry are rewarded with a very special time of Christian fellowship. Preparation for these four weekends goes on for the entire year, as guest speakers, music, meals, accommodations, premium gifts, and a thousand and one other details are painstakingly checked off the master list.

And Friday afternoon, when the guests arrive, they simply check in and enjoy it all. Unmindful, I'm sure, of how much work it has taken to create the delightful ambience that seems to effortlessly surround the group.

Friends, let us never forget the effort it has taken to unlock heaven's doors for the grand opening. Not just the construction of mansions, the paving of streets, or the lush landscaping and table settings.

But most of all, a magnificent effort one weekend 2,000 years ago.

Heavenly Diamonds

8

Acre upon acre of beautifully manicured softball fields. Shimmering green grass cut to regulation length. Base lines and batters' boxes carefully marked out in glistening white chalk. A roll of factory-fresh softballs still in their Spalding boxes. A rack of new Power Alley aluminum bats in each dugout.

And a league schedule that runs 52 weeks a year.

That, my friend, is what heaven is going to be like.

* * *

For years the issue of softball-in-heaven has been hotly debated throughout Christendom. Well, maybe not that hotly. And maybe not all that widely. But it's time someone laid this question to rest for all time, and why shouldn't I be the one to do it? *There will be softball in heaven.* End of discussion.

Is it hard for you to imagine your home in heaven with a neatly laundered softball uniform in the closet? Taking it down and meticulously suiting up for the afternoon game—jersey, baseball pants, socks, stirrups, batting glove, cap, and mitt? Walking out the front door of your mansion and jogging over to the nearby field, greeting new friends along the way? Taking your familiar spot in left field for the bottom of the first inning? Going three for four in a close 9-7 game?

Why can't heaven be that real and that delightful? I've grown weary—all of us have—of the dreary picture of heaven so often presented as enticement to clean living. Clouds, robes, harps. That's *heaven?* Not much to last one afternoon, let alone eternity.

My friend Steve Mosley, in one of his outstanding *It Is Written* television scripts entitled "Heaven's Borderline," describes a saint looking over the "traditional" heaven upon arrival. After one quick glance at the sterile paradise, he mutters to himself, "I wish I'd brought a magazine."

I can just imagine the printed daily schedule of events as anticipated by some saints:

7:00 a.m.	Breakfast (manna, selected fruits in season)
8:00 a.m.	Group harp lesson in temple courtyard
9:30 a.m.	Angel harp concert (also musical solos on sackbut, dulcimer, and psaltery)
11:00 a.m.	Practice period (harp)
12:00 noon	Lunch (harp-shaped manna hors d'oeuvres)
1:00 p.m.	Free period (standing around in white ankle-length robes, sitting beside tame lions, shielding eyes from glare of golden streets)
2:00 p.m.	Arts and crafts (stringing and retuning harps)
3:00 p.m.	Second half of Angel Harp Concert Double Bill
5:00 p.m.	Banquet with harp accompaniment
6:00 p.m.-7:00 a.m.	Marathon harp playing (remember, there's no night there)

Oh, boy! It takes a certain amount of pluck to stay enthusiastic about that lineup for long.

But what about softball? And half-court basketball? What about Frisbees and growing our own masterpiece gardens? What about blue jeans and cherry cheesecake and chewing gum and octophonic CD players?

* * *

I love the heaven described by Deborah Anfenson-Vance in her essay "In the Surprising By and By."

"Today I gave a good share of my writing time to baking cookies with my 4-year-old daughter. We had fun and made a mess. I can't think of one good reason we won't be able to do the same thing in heaven, providing we don't eat too much raw cookie dough."

She goes on to suggest a heaven, not just with cookies, but with pizza and enchiladas as well. A heaven with ethnic differences and cultures—now loved and appreciated by all its citizens. A heaven with wildly delicious varieties and surprises.

Author and youth minister Steve Marshall writes in his delightful book *Grandma on the Sea of Glass* about the effervescent reality of heaven. Skydiving. Multicolored robes that change to paisley polka dots on a moment's notice. Little old grandmas jumping the tiny waves on the edge of the sea of glass. Sights and smells and sounds and tastes that will exhilarate the senses for delightful ages.

It will all be so *real.*

That's one concept that's somehow hard to accept. Heaven will be real! Satisfyingly real. Day after day, month after month, year after year will fly by in a whirlwind of ever-growing and satisfying reality.

I used to think of heaven as a place where all God's saints possessed—and smugly exploited—magical creative powers. Residents would wander around the golden streets declaring, "I want a *this!* I want a *that!*" Then with a blink of the eyes or a twitch of the nose, the requested item would appear out of the clear blue. New mansions. New suits. (Robes, I mean.) Purple giraffes to play with. (I was 8 when I used to think this way.)

Now I begin to see how shallow and unsatisfying that would be. How much more rewarding to work and study and design and plan for the goals and dreams we want to accomplish! Unhampered by time constraints, unlimited in our mental resources and physical dexterity, our capacity and energy and zest for *doing* constantly grow and advance.

(Of course, if company's coming over and we're late preparing dinner, it might still be nice to blink my eyes and have the table set for supper. So who knows?)

The sixty-fifth chapter of Isaiah is a too-often-forgotten reminder that life there will be wonderfully real. There will be an active construction business, says verse 21. We will build houses and live in them. Planting and farming and gardening will be challenging and rewarding enterprises. "My chosen ones will long *enjoy* the works of their hands" (verse 22, NIV).

Have you ever worked all day and had your energy level stay high from beginning to end? had every project turn out right? been able to look back at 5:00 p.m. and say with quiet satisfaction, *"I did this"*? We'll enjoy that kind of stimulating experience in heaven *every day!*

And if, after such a satisfying day of productive challenges, we head to the softball fields for the camaraderie of a good game, what could be more right?

* * *

There are objections—legitimate objections—that one might raise. What about competition? The hurt feelings that come from losing? The desire to excel at the expense of another? The problems of temper and angry words spoken in the heat of a close call at home plate?

I have wrestled with these, both on the ball field and here at my desk, thinking and writing. The only answer I can come up with is this: Imagine Jesus as a player on that softball field.

When I picture Jesus playing ball in heaven, I begin to think that it is possible to play the game in a Christian manner. Unfortunately, I have never seen Him play. All I have to go by is the play of Christians who are trying to live like Him.

A number of years ago I played in a Christian summer league. I especially remember the behavior of one new team. They argued every decision. They called people names. They flung their gloves and crabbed at the umpires. On any close play, three or four would run in from the outfield, ready to share a piece of their mind. "No way! Come on, ump! Read the rulebook! Protest the game!" On and on.

But time went by. The spirit of Christ worked in their hearts. Several seasons later, you wouldn't have recognized these fellows. A miracle had taken place.

They still loved to win; don't get me wrong. But they had learned to love the simple zest of playing the game even more, and they had learned to love the Lord Jesus best of all.

They never argued close calls anymore. They just nodded with a smile and went on to the next hitter. They cheered each other on . . . and the opposing players, too. When they popped up with the bases loaded, they just grinned, grabbed their gloves, and trotted out to their positions. When an opposing player made a good play, they congratulated him with absolute sincerity. They prayed a lot. They witnessed incessantly.

It was as though these 15 young men had decided that they were going to glorify God in everything they did on that field. It was a beautiful and moving thing to see.

Unfortunately, they still beat our team a lot; but it was worth it just to spend those two hours with them. I guess.

And if we can get that close to heaven's ideal playing softball down here, when we finally arrive up there, by the grace of God we can pull it off! I'm convinced of it.

Softball in heaven.

Let me say this with all humility: there's a chance I'm wrong. Very slight, to be sure. But even with all the vehemence I expressed earlier, mathematically speaking, there is the possibility that when we arrive and look around, the expected row of softball diamonds will not be there.

But only because something better is there in its place. Right now I can't imagine what it could be. But there's this small chance that God's creative powers will have come up with some activity so much grander that softball simply won't be worth playing anymore.

* * *

I used to love driving the little cars at Disneyland's Autorama. The night before a trip to the Magic Kingdom, I would lie awake anticipating my rides around the track in a little red hot rod.

I don't do that anymore. Now that I have a real garage with a real car in it that can barrel down the highway at a hot 55 mph, the Autorama hot rods aren't that big a deal.

I'm willing to be open to the possibility that many of

heaven's surprises will be so grand that our cherished dreams and favorite activities will shatter into obsolescence. Even softball.

Jesus once told cynical onlookers that in heaven the institution of marriage will be no more. For 2,000 years since that pronouncement, people have worried about it. *I've* worried about it.

But I've begun to stop fretting. Every fresh glimpse I get into the character of God assures me that He is capable of providing us with new kinds of relationships that will satisfy us even more than what we have down here, fulfilling though our present experiences may be for the moment.

Friendships closer than marriage. Caring and tender relationships more gratifying than even the sexual unions that are so comforting in this cruel earth.

Hard to imagine? Yes. But possible to accept and anticipate.

One truth about heaven that I believe is ironclad: any expected pleasure that is missing will be replaced by something that is better. No exceptions.

What? No macaroni-and-cheese dinners? Something better instead. No Cosby show? Something much funnier and more entertaining. No waterbeds? Something far more restful must be waiting in its place.

Go ahead and imagine what heaven will be like. But be prepared to be surprised . . . always pleasantly surprised. Every missing ingredient will be replaced elegantly with something vastly better, unquestionably more delightful.

If there's a recreation good enough to replace softball, heaven is where we will learn to play it. If there are foods tasty enough to displace your current favorites, they will be on God's menu. Count on Him to deliver without once failing.

One more confident and whimsical observation from Debbie Anfenson-Vance: "Human imagination, even in a sinful, deathful world, has produced, for good or evil, what seems beyond imagination. Beethoven's Sixth Symphony. Nuclear fission. The Sears Tower. Laser surgery. The Greek plays. Compact disks. New York City. Microwave ovens.

Florence, Italy. Smart cars. Dove Bars.

"If we see these things now, coming from a society limited by time, evil, mistrust, disease, and itself, what might we see in a new earth? Certainly the sweet by and by won't be the scene of stifled creativity and inactive imaginations. *And what might come from the imagination of the One who created us to create?*

"My ideas of heaven may be all mixed up," she admits. "I'm just a kid sitting under the Christmas tree, rattling packages and making guesses. I hear things when I jiggle the boxes, but I won't be sure of anything till I've opened the presents."

One thing's for sure: it's going to be a terrific Christmas.

The Complaining Aliens

9

Everyone's against us!"
Lately it's the common cry of Christendom. In the past decade or so, evangelical America has developed a persecution complex that seems to be growing, especially during election years.

"Public school textbooks don't teach what we want them to teach." "School boards and the Supreme Court won't let us have organized prayers." "We pay taxes to support a humanistic school system but can't get tuition tax assistance from Uncle Sam for our Christian schools." "We can't have a cardboard Mary and the Baby Jesus on the steps of City Hall at Christmastime." "The government subsidizes abortions and *Playboy* subscriptions in our military PXs." "Sex education is a conspiracy by left-wing Planned Parenthooders."

And so on.

As a conservative Christian myself, I have two observations that may surprise you:

* * *

First, *what else did you expect?*
Christians are, first and foremost, citizens of the better land. Do we really expect things to go our way down here in alien territory? More on that a little later.

Second, *thank God things are the way they are!* Now I really have you going, haven't I?

I readily accept the label. I'm an evangelical, Bible-believing, gung-ho Christian activist. I also heartily agree with 1984 presidential candidate Walter Mondale, who said so eloquently, "Today the First Amendment clauses do not need to be fixed; they need to be followed."

Amen.

Today too many Christians—members of the most potent and proven faith system the world has ever seen—want the government to help their religion. They want Congress to bolster their evangelistic efforts. They expect the Supreme Court to assist in their witness.

Let me say it plainly: *Christianity is the one religion that doesn't need that kind of help.* It's the one faith that can stand on its own two feet, and it's always flourished best when allowed to do just that.

Take this business of school prayer. Today as I write this, any schoolchild in the nation can bow his or her head and say a prayer. "Jesus, bless this food." "Jesus, help me to remember how to do this math problem." "Jesus, please be with Bill, who just lost his dad." Honest, open, unmemorized, powerful little prayers. And all the Supreme Court justices, school board chairpersons, and American Civil Liberties Union societies in the world cannot stop him.

On the other hand, teachers who are paid by the state cannot get up front and say, "Now, class, we are going to pray. Everyone bow your head as we recite. And by the way, anyone who doesn't believe in praying can wait out in the hall."

Deep in our hearts, we know it would be wrong for our government to *direct* students in prayer. It's wrong to write state prayers and wrong to force kids to say them. It's wrong to allow that kind of pressure to exist in our pluralistic society.

Picture the little Jewish boy standing out in the hallway, tears glistening in his eyes. Inside, the other children are parroting a "voluntary" Christian prayer, so he is left out. Later, during recess, he endures the jibes of kids who don't know better. "What's the matter with you?" "Don't you believe in God?" His parents get anonymous mail: "Go back where you came from."

Don't kid yourself; the "pro-prayer" movement is really a "pro-*Christian* prayers" movement. If the floodgates were truly opened, and we had a steady stream of Buddhist chants, Hindu incantations, Moonie monologues, atheist anthems, Mormon theology, and sacrilegious high school valley girl snicker-filled prayers across the nation, there'd be a repeal movement going before the first week was out.

The heart of the tragedy is that the school prayer movement would shut down genuine prayer and substitute vapid, meaningless, little two-line rhymes in its place. Remember the student who for years wondered why everyone was chanting "Lead us not into Penn Station."

* * *

Evangelical Christian Chuck Colson, who is no friend of the ACLU, writes compellingly about this matter of school prayer in his outstanding book *Kingdoms in Conflict.* He admits his is a minority position, but calls the movement a "Trojan horse."

"Who does the organizing?" he asks. "If it is the school board, Caesar is being given a spiritual function; admittedly a small crack in the door, but a crack nonetheless. I for one don't want my grandchildren reciting prayers determined by government officials. And in actual practice they would be so watered down as to be of no effect except perhaps to water down my grandchildren's growing faith."

How true that it does run contrary to our instincts for citizens of heaven to "vote against prayer." May God help us to keep our perspective! We are not voting against prayer, but against government-enforced religious formalities and state intrusion into pure faith. We cannot outlaw true prayer any more than we can "kick God out of the classroom." I've always resented that phrase; what kind of gutless God would allow Himself to be booted out of a brick building by our ballots? Heaven's citizens know their God is more omnipotent than that!

Let me say it once more: Christian faith simply doesn't need government help! Colson again: "The Christian, knowing that the will of the majority cannot determine truth, seeks no preferential favor for his religion from government. His confidence, instead, is that truth is found in Christ alone—and this is so no matter how many people believe it, no matter whether those in power believe it. While this may sound exclusivistic, it is this very assurance that makes (or should make, when properly understood) the Christian the most vigorous defender of human liberty."

* * *

It can sometimes be costly to take this no-help, thanks-anyway attitude. But it is one of the Christian's noblest challenges as he seeks to keep his faith uncorrupted.

I speak from experience. For 10 years now, I—a tax-paying American citizen—have shelled out thousands of dollars a year for tuition for my two daughters. Why don't I clamor for tuition tax credits or vouchers or rebates?

Because I don't want them. It would be wrong for me to accept them.

Here's why: Day in and day out my girls go to Christian schools and hear about Jesus Christ. Not just in Bible class, but in mathematics, in science (where they freely hear creationism, by the way), in English and spelling, and even in PE, Jesus Christ and His answers for daily living are cheerfully pumped into my two daughters seven hours a day, five days a week, 180 days a year. Their Christian schools open with prayer, they close with prayer, they seem to pray all the way through the middle, too.

Now, would it really be right for my nonbelieving neighbors to be forced to help subsidize that? No way!

I'd be stealing if I accepted government money to fund that kind of Christian educating. I don't want the money, I don't want the strings attached, I don't want Uncle Sam's involvement in any way . . . except perhaps to make sure there are enough fire extinguishers on the walls and that the teachers know not only Jesus Christ but also their nouns, verbs, and times tables.

Is it double taxation? You bet! And I'm glad to pay it! Christian education is worth every penny. And I would say to activist parents who keep griping about humanistic textbooks and evolution and mandated school prayer, "Instead of expecting government to do everything your way, why not invest in the kind of education you really want?"

It's just like the couple who decides to pay out of their own pocket for a Christian church wedding instead of the free "justice of the peace" variety. It's double taxation, to be sure, and we voluntarily choose it if that's what we care about.

"Thanks, but no thanks." Somehow it's a lot harder to say that than to claim "We were here first" or "We know what's right . . . for us and for all of you too."

* * *

I've encountered the "we were here first" mentality at Christian gatherings more times than I can count. Sometimes it's called the "Christian nation" concept—"This is a 'Christian nation,' so we should have things our way: Christian prayers, Christian laws, Christian leaders."

One more slice of Colson wisdom, if you please: "America is not the New Jerusalem or a 'city upon a hill,' though some of its founders harbored that vision. Nor are Americans God's chosen people. The kingdom of God is universal, bound by neither race nor nation. But Abraham Lincoln used an interesting phrase; Americans, he said, were the 'almost chosen people.' If there is any justification for that term—not theologically but historically—it is because in the hammering out of a new republic, the combination of wisdom, reason, and providence produced a church-state relationship that uniquely respected the differing roles of each."

Roland Hegstad, editor of *Liberty* magazine, suggests that America is blessed, not because she is a "Christian nation" or has "Christian laws," but precisely because she has always respected and set into her foundation that hallmark of freedom—liberty of conscience. Sadly ironic, perhaps, that God has blessed our country precisely because of that wall that many Christians are trying to tear down today.

And God Himself often steps in to protect His wall.

* * *

Morris Venden tells of an experience in his book *Here I Come, Ready or Not*. A group of religious and civic leaders in Phoenix, Arizona, were preparing to pass a Sunday "blue law" that would close businesses in an attempt to foster a religious environment. One thoughtful pastor appealed to his conference religious liberty director for assistance in opposing the group's well-known lawyer.

"When the lawyer showed up," Venden writes, "he was so eloquent and presented his case with such apparent logic that the group was convinced to follow his suggestions and proceed with definite moves in the direction of enforcing the Sunday blue laws.

"The local pastor thought he should say something to try to counteract the lawyer's presentation, but when he stood up to speak, he found himself unable to say a word. He said that his whole mouth felt like it was full of cotton. After trying for a few moments, he gave up and sat down.

"Elder Johns [the lawyer who had come with the pastor] then decided it was up to him to save the day, so he stood up. When they compared notes later, they found that they both experienced the same inability to speak. Elder Johns' mouth also went dry, and he was not able to say a word.

"As they slumped in their seats, wondering what was going on, the door opened and in walked a man in a pin-striped business suit. He approached the microphone and said, 'I am a citizen, and I would like to say something.' And in a few paragraphs he made the lawyer's arguments look like nothing. The place became deathly still. The lawyer attempted to refute his arguments but was obviously confused, and the meeting ended in confusion.

"Elder Johns and the local pastor tried to find the man in the business suit at the close of the meeting, but he was gone! You would expect that, wouldn't you? He was gone. Elder Johns told me that in all of his 40 years of ministry, he had never had a more inspiring moment than that one."

God has a vision for government, doesn't He? He has shared that vision with His people, and He has shared heaven's resources to help preserve that kind of liberty.

"Render unto Caesar that which is Caesar's, and unto God that which is God's," said Jesus, and so it is in our own First Amendment. "By refusing to assign redemptive powers to the state or to allow coercive power to the church, the American experiment separated these two institutions for the first time since Constantine," says Colson. And I pray that thoughtful Christians will ever rise up to oppose any shallow-minded attempts to weaken that amendment or that wall of separation that has served so well for two centuries.

The tough question is this: *What, then, do we do?* How should we act?

* * *

Should heaven's citizens adopt the "just passing through" mentality? Do we forget about voting, about community involvement, about concern over moral issues? "Any day now, I'll be raptured, so the world can just go its own way"?

On the other hand, do we try to take over in the name of God? Up till now, this has been our greater temptation.

What do we do? Truly we live amid "kingdoms in conflict."

If you've not already purchased a copy of *Kingdoms in Conflict,* I would encourage you to do so. Its insights are must reading for thinking Christians of the nineties.

"The church, while not the kingdom of God, is to live out the values of the kingdom of God in this world, resisting the ever-present temptation to usher in the kingdom of God by political means. Yet this is the temptation to which the church has most commonly succumbed, and certainly this is its greatest temptation today."

"No one can be coerced into true faith, and the last people who even ought to try to do so are Christians, either individually or as members of the institutional church."

"The Christian's goal is not to strive to rule, but to be ruled."

"God commands His people to influence the world through their obedience to Him, not by taking over the world through the corridors of power."

74

"Laws are most often reformed as a result of powerful spiritual movements. I know of no case where a spiritual movement was achieved by passing laws. . . . Christian citizens should be activists about their faith, striving by their witness to 'Christianize' their culture—not by the force of the sword, but by the force of their ideas."

"It is, in fact, their dual citizenship that should, as Augustine believed, make Christians the best of citizens. Not because they are more patriotic or civic-minded, but because they do out of obedience to God that which others do only if they choose or if they are forced. And their very presence in society means the presence of a community of people who live by the Law behind the law."

"Christian patriots spend more time washing feet than waving flags. . . . It's difficult to stand on a pedestal and wash the feet of those below."

Washing the feet of our fellowman. Being the salt of the earth by caring and sharing. In chapter after chapter of that great book and its companion volume, *Loving God,* Colson tells of men and women who are making a difference in this world simply by doing what they can do for others. "Little platoons," he calls them. People who, while citizens of heaven, are giving 110 percent during their temporary exile here on earth. Winning small battles that are part of God's great victory.

We live in two kingdoms by loving God, and we love Him by loving our fellowman and loving our country. We do what we can—prayerfully. We vote—prayerfully. We may even, on occasion, march or picket—prayerfully. Always with our focus on heaven and our ultimate citizenship there.

One of these days we will leave our country and this tired old planet behind. We will finally bid farewell to a government that at last has embraced and enforced the religious tyranny described in Revelation 13: "He had power to give life unto the image of the beast, that the image of the beast should both speak, and cause that as many as would not worship the image of the beast should be killed" (verse 15).

Those who don't worship in a certain prescribed way will

75

be executed. That's the final solution nations and governments will adopt in the last days.

And in the end God rescues His heavenly citizens from that terror. But as we escape from this earthly kingdom now gone desperately mad, as we are "caught up together . . . in the clouds," perhaps we will look back with mixed emotions. May we be known as visitors and aliens who served well while we could.

New Eyes, New Heart

10

It was a warm June evening in the college gymnasium. Rows of folding metal chairs set up for graduation covered the immense hardwood floor and its faded basketball/ volleyball markings. I shifted uncomfortably in my seat as the list of names droned on.

I was there at my alma mater with my wife and relatives to see my sister-in-law receive her diploma. Pacific Union College is a Christian liberal arts college in Angwin (where?), up in the Napa wine country of northern California. Four years after my own graduation, I still recognized a number of the professors on the platform. Occasionally a familiar name would echo through the loudspeakers as a younger brother or sister of one of my peers would step forward.

The mood of the evening was definitely relaxed, almost secular, now that the invocation and commencement address were over. Smatterings of applause from small knots of relatives accompanied most names; every now and then a favorite student or honors graduate would get a fairly sustained ripple of clapping.

Of course, there were explosions of flash cameras and an occasional whoop or good-natured catcall from some wise guy in the back. "Fraud! Fraud!" "Remember the raid!" (Inside joke, apparently.)

Finally, Merry walked up to receive her parchment, and I settled back to endure the final batch of remaining names. The remote bits of scattered clapping continued.

Suddenly a wave of steady applause began to roll through the gymnasium. Not a wave, really, but a thunder. I glanced up with some renewed interest. The class president? Dean's daughter? Some senior who had rescued a kid from drowning last week?

* * *

I was startled to notice a young lady I recognized from my own student days. This many years later, she was finally graduating. Not an officer, not a dean's list student. I couldn't even remember her name, yet the ovation was swelling to a roar as this very ordinary girl made her way across the platform.

Her white cane tapped out the way to the table where the college president stood waiting with her diploma in his outstretched hand.

For a moment time stood still. A flood of insight hit me as I began to comprehend what this moment represented to that young girl.

Pacific Union College is built on a hill. There are steps leading to *everything*. Steps to the dorm, to the library, to the cafeteria, to the college market, to the classroom complexes spread out over this intricate campus. Winding paths and narrow sidewalks and slippery, rain-slicked roads.

And this girl was blind.

I thought about my own five years of tough classes in a bachelor's and master's program. Frantic note-taking in class. Studying late at night. Term papers and projects. Labs. And I could see!

Then I thought about the many pleasures that went along with the rigors of college life. Lazy afternoons on hikes with a new girlfriend. Spectacular sunsets and lengthening shadows across the symmetrical row of tennis courts. Film discussions and waterskiing. So many visual treasures that helped soften the Spartan life. So many treasures that only a sighted person could experience.

Somehow this little champion of a girl had made it without those things. Somehow in her darkness she had finished what most of us barely can limp through with two good eyes.

I could sense that similar thoughts were flashing through every person's mind in that massive auditorium. As the poignant reality of this girl's accomplishment shuddered through the group, applause was no longer good enough. We rose as one person to our feet. The standing ovation went on for five minutes.

For one helpless moment, I tried to hold back the tears. Then I gave up and just let them flow. So did everybody there. It was one of the most touching memories I will ever carry.

These many years later, I leafed reverently through a yearbook to learn her name. Shirley. I have no idea where she is today, but, Shirley, thank you for what you did for me. I will never forget that evening.

But even after the applause died down and the damp-eyed audience sank back into their seats, Shirley stayed blind. During the postgrad parties, all she could see was darkness. One week later, one year later, now a decade later, she is still coping somehow with the pain of a midnight-black world. When she puts on her socks, as she looks for jobs, as she tries to build some kind of social life, she is still blind.

Blind.

What a word. What is it like to be *blind?* I once asked my ninth- and tenth-grade Bible class to imagine they were blind. With their eyes closed, they tried to enter that world. The pain, the frustration, the empty void, the almost shattering limitations.

Then they wrote their feelings for me. With pinched, frightened faces, these suddenly sober students poured out their emotions of fear and rage in a torrent of bitterness—over an imagined experience that was blithely temporary.

Blind. Try, if you can, to experience the darkness of being blind.

And then comes heaven.

* * *

One day soon all the Shirleys of the world will see. Some of them will see *again;* others will see for the very first time. Finally, after such a long wait in the dark, they will see the face of Jesus, who has just healed them.

Someday, someway, God Himself will make it all up to those who have borne the heaviest measure of this demonic demonstration called sin. Up until now, the distribution of agony has been anything but fair, but God will make it right then. Those who cannot see today will see then with exquisite vividness the visual paradise that is heaven.

And even you and I who can see to read this page surely can long a little more earnestly for that day of healing to come soon.

The Bible talks about the blind being healed. The deaf will hear. The lame man will leap as a hart.

* * *

But there's one tragedy too often unmentioned in the list. I have a little niece who is mentally disabled. For years now she and her parents have walked that painful road. Special schools. Remedial therapy. In a thousand and one ways every day that tragedy has touched their lives.

And of course there are the endless repetitions and the frustrations of sensing that so many messages of love are just not getting through.

But then comes heaven. The blind will see, the lame will walk, and all the connections will suddenly be "hooked up right" in so many children. "In the twinkling of an eye," little eyes will suddenly brim with brand-new intelligence.

What a gift—and what a day—that will be!

Just last weekend I was the guest speaker at a church in southern California. During the Bible study period, I sat behind a middle-aged man who was mentally disabled. My heart still aches.

He turned around in his seat and looked at me through heavy rims. He held out a hand for me to shake. "How're you?" he mumbled.

A few minutes later he turned around again and held out his hand once more. "How're you?"

As the group studied the Bible together, he gazed around the small room, grunting to himself. Every time the class looked up a text, he thrust a Bible into my hands. "Look it up," he whispered hoarsely. I would quickly find the verse for him, hand the Bible back, and leaf through my own copy for the text. Not glancing at the passage, he would stare intently into space until the next Scripture text. Then the same instructions: "Look it up."

He was dressed shabbily with stained blue pants and a shirt that was untucked in the back. Several inches of underwear peeked out from the top of the trousers. He had this frightful habit of picking at his nose, inspecting whatever he found, and then sucking on his finger. I shuddered. Would the lesson never end?

In spite of myself, I longed to get out of there. I was eager to escape from this man's presence and get up on the platform and preach about God's love.

I couldn't help sensing the irony of those conflicting desires. Several times during that hour, I prayed silently, "Lord, help me to love this man as You love him."

Somehow God gave me just a slice of understanding into that poor man's existence. I saw through his eyes—the fog of confusion, the frightening maze of his mental limitations. What is only an irritant to us is numbing pain and fear to him.

I finished my sermon, shook hands with everyone, and drove home to my happy, healthy family. He went home too. Somehow he must continue on . . .

And then comes heaven. The trumpets will sound, and Jesus will come. And in one triumphant moment, that man will stand up straight and tall with clear eyes that suddenly are capable of taking it all in. The glassy gaze will be transformed into a 20/20 vision of heaven's bright reality. That poor disabled man will be made brand-new.

"Behold, I make *all* things new."

* * *

Whatever the damage done, Jesus will make us new.

Twisted limbs. Diseases. Disfigurements and amputated legs. Jesus will make us new.

Radical mastectomies and malfunctioning heart valves. Jesus will make us new.

Even our minor maladies will be miraculously cared for by our returning Saviour who misses no detail. Glasses and contact lenses and hearing aids and orthodontia will be left in the dust. Unshapely noses will be transformed. Jesus will make us new.

And new hearts. I want a new heart most of all. One of my favorite gospel hymns begins like this: "Soon and very soon, we are going to see the King. Hallelujah! Hallelujah! We're going to see the King!" A new King, a new home, new friends, a new city.

And He makes all things new.

Especially people.

God, let it be soon.

Goodbye, Daddy

11

A few chapters ago I told you about my grandfather, Elder Dan Venden, who passed away in 1973. Now, as we close, allow me to share with you the rest of the story.

I was a freshman attending Pacific Union College with my older brother Dan. My folks were completing one more term of mission service in Thailand. We were lucky that my grandparents lived just eight miles down the hill.

I still remember driving with Dan in his little blue VW to visit them. Generally unannounced . . . and always around suppertime. They never complained about our barging in, and I must say—to our credit—that we always did the dishes afterward.

Very early in 1973, the doctor's diagnosis came in: cancer. I had never seen up close what this disease can do to a man. In Grandpa's case, it took its toll in a hurry.

Only a missionary family can truly comprehend the quandary my mother found herself in, 12,000 miles away from her dying father.

Even just those few years ago, overseas telephone calls were not the directly dialed miracles they are today. Communication was difficult; overseas letters seemed to crawl back and forth across the Pacific.

Finally in May she decided to come home. I remember picking her up in San Francisco and pulling into the driveway of the familiar house in St. Helena.

With his daughter near, Grandpa seemed to take a turn for the better. Ever so slight, but his condition seemed to stabilize. Several weeks went by before he began to weaken again.

Mom found herself in the agonizing predicament of waiting for something to happen. Out in the mission field, a husband and two younger sons needed her. Right here close at hand, it was beginning to look like the end . . . but perhaps not for a while yet.

What to do?

More time went by. I remember painful discussions with Mom and Dan about what she should do. A funeral might still be weeks, even months, away.

Finally she made up her mind. "I've got to go back." She booked her return flight and prepared to say goodbye.

The day came. Mom and Grandpa had one final private visit, one last prayer together. Then came that wrenching moment when she said goodbye to him. That last goodbye.

For weeks I had dreaded it. Mom was a crybaby at heart; I had visions of emotional collapse. I steeled myself for the worst.

Grandpa was in the living room on the sofa. Lying there, he could look out the picture window and see the driveway and the road leading to the highway.

Mom checked her bags one last time and hugged all the relatives. "I guess this is it," she said evenly. She turned to her dad.

Sitting on the edge of the sofa, she took his hand for the last time. It didn't hit me until later that she *knew* it was the last time.

"Well, goodbye, Daddy," she said with a calmness that hit me like a ton of bricks. "I'll see you later."

"Goodbye, Jean," he responded. "I'll see you." She squeezed his hand, stood up, and walked out the door. As she walked past the picture window to the car, she waved at him again.

He raised his hand tentatively and murmured "Goodbye" before she disappeared from view.

* * *

As we drove to the airport I kept stealing furtive glances at Mom. A little red around the eyes, but composed. I didn't understand it.

At the airline terminal, she said goodbye to the rest of us. I was already scheduled to fly out a week later, so that part was not difficult. She gave Grandma a long hug; they seemed to draw strength from each other.

"You're such a brick," Mom murmured.

"Well, we'll be OK," Grandma replied. "You get back to your family, Jean."

Moments later she was gone. As we drove back to St. Helena I thought about my mother, now sitting in that airplane all alone with her thoughts. I wondered about that final conversation she had shared with her dad.

* * *

One week later.

Grandpa was now in the hospital. We stopped there on my way to the airport.

I had dreaded this moment too. In all honesty, I was a giddy-minded college punk; yet I still was capable of sensing what we all were about to lose. I did not like the idea of saying my last goodbye to Grandpa.

I stood at the side of his bed and told him I loved him. He didn't notice the haircut I had gotten just for him, but still had the strength to grin when I pointed it out. "You call that a haircut?" he responded, his voice thin. "You ought to let me have a go at it."

We talked for several minutes. Then he motioned me closer. "Let's pray before you go."

No one could pray like my grandpa. It was a precious final memory.

Out in the hallway I leaned against the wall. For just one moment I struggled to keep my teenage emotions in check. "Let's go," I said at last, picking up my suitcase.

One week later, out in Thailand, on a Sunday afternoon, we returned home to find a telegram taped to our doorway. "Let me get it," Dad said soberly. He glanced at it, then handed it wordlessly to my mother.

Grandpa was gone.

Yes, we did shed some tears that day. But I was still intrigued and quietly impressed by my mother's fortitude during that earlier day of farewells. Not until years later did I ask Mom what she had said to her dad in that last private conversation. She sat for a moment, thinking.

"It was nothing, really," she said at last. "I guess I just said to him, 'Daddy, you know how much I love you and hope you get well. But if you don't, I'll meet you in heaven. We'll be together again then.'"

At last I understood.

* * *

I don't know what heaven means to you, but I can tell you what it means to my family. *No more goodbyes.*

Never again. Not once ever again will we go through the pain of saying goodbye to those we love.

As I review in my mind our family's history of missionary service, it's those goodbyes that stick out in my memory. Like the red light on a police cruiser, they point out the pain of traveling down earth's road.

I remember our family driving along DeWitt Drive in north Hollywood on our way to Los Angeles International Airport for another four-year stint. Moments earlier we had just said goodbye to my grandparents. My other grandparents.

And my memory is of seeing my dad brush away tears in a sudden and very rare burst of emotion. Dad crying! That really got to me.

"I hate this!" I remember him muttering to Mom, his voice shaking. "I hate leaving them!"

She didn't say anything, just took his hand and held it. If anyone understood goodbyes . . .

* * *

May 1970. Singapore International Airport. My brother Dan and I were leaving boarding school three weeks early to return to the States. A faculty member drove us to the airport, with the good wishes of an envious student body ringing in our ears.

Sitting next to me in the car was my girlfriend, Margie. Far

Eastern Academy was one school where young romances were nipped in the bud every year by families returning to faraway mission destinations or home to the States. A compassionate staff seemed to understand the pain of even these teen tragedies.

I was barely 15, and she was two months younger. But I won't forget that last walk—starkly quiet—through the airline terminal before we said goodbye. The chaperoning teacher graciously looked the other way as I gave Margie a clumsy kiss. (Let certain parties make the most of this admission!) Today it's a sweet memory. But it sure hurt then.

The very next evening friends in Bangkok gathered to bid my parents farewell. I was there, and to this day a song remains in my mind: "Till We Meet Again," sung by a diminutive Thai man named Tong Inn. Many years earlier, my folks had helped arrange for him to receive life-saving surgery at our mission hospital in Bangkok. Later he took Bible studies from them and gave his life to the Lord.

Now he sang those words, "Till we meet, till we meet, till we meet at Jesus' feet," in a strained tenor voice trembling with emotion. After the service he said goodbye to Mom and Dad. "You saved my life," he repeated several times. "I'll be faithful; you can count on me. We will meet again."

Now, when Dad's a guest in other churches, he regularly preaches a sermon titled "Jewels From Thailand." Tong Inn was one jewel it was difficult to leave.

*   *   *

August 1972. Dan and I had just *returned* from Los Angeles International Airport. The rest of the family had headed overseas again, leaving Dan and me behind to attend college.

I was trying to get to sleep that night when the loneliness came pounding into my soul. In a rush it hit me how far away Mom and Dad were going to be, how long it was going to be before we'd be together again.

For the longest hour I was 17 going on 5. I cried like a little kid, huddled alone in a sleeping bag on the floor of my grandparents' home. The pain of saying goodbye hurt like everything.

Many years later Dan told me how he had slipped out that same evening and gone for a long walk by himself. He experienced the same crushing rush of despair sitting on a curb several blocks away; somehow he wrestled his emotions back into control before returning to the house.

Goodbyes. Our souls are scarred with them.

But one day soon comes the Reunion. And then we will say with heartfelt gratitude ringing in our voices: "Never part again!"

* * *

May 25, 1989.–Jessica's funeral.

Jessica was just 40 years old when she passed away. She and her husband had both worked at the same Christian ministry. Monday morning they went for their usual walk together during the 10:00 break. Coworkers saw them holding hands and chatting. She went home early, however, complaining of fatigue. She got up at noon to fix a lunch for her teenage son and then rested some more.

A few hours later she quietly died alone in her living room easy chair. A weakened heart had suddenly had enough.

At 5:00 that evening, unaware of the fresh tragedy, I picked up my daughter at school. Her eyes were red.

"We need to pray for Matt," she said to me quietly. "He just lost his mom."

It took me a moment to put it together. *Matt's mom was Joe's wife.*

Fear in my heart, I drove to their house. Could it be a mistake?

There in his driveway was a police car.

The next few days we did what we could to help. Funeral arrangements, casseroles, flowers, words of comfort. For the first time in my life I found myself right in the middle of this painful process.

Finally we sat together in the church as a spiritual family, listening to words of hope. "For the Lord himself shall descend from heaven with a shout, with the voice of the archangel, and with the trump of God: and the dead in Christ shall rise first: then we which are alive and remain shall be caught up together with them in the clouds, to meet the Lord in the air: and so shall we ever be with the Lord. Wherefore comfort one another with these words" (1 Thessalonians 4:16-18).

I wonder if even God Himself knew how often we would draw comfort from those words! That hope saw us through that long Thursday afternoon.

* * *

It was sometime during that week, as I searched for truth to sustain my friend, that I remembered an earlier experience of my own. For 10 difficult months I had commuted to a new job away from my family. Early Monday morning I would get up at 4:45 a.m., eat a bowl of cold cereal, then drive 130 miles to work. Staying all week with my brother, I would drive home Friday afternoon for a weekend with my family.

It was an unusual life, and I experienced a weekly cycle of emotional turmoil.

I loved the weekends. But around Sunday morning the thought would begin to gnaw at me: *Tomorrow you head back to work.* I almost couldn't enjoy my weekend at home, thinking about the goodbye so soon to come.

On the other hand, during the week at work, I had that reunion to look forward to. Around Wednesday afternoon the mental countdown would begin in the other direction: *Friday will be here soon!*

On Friday afternoon fellow workers climbed casually into their cars and drove home. Ho-hum. No big deal. But not me! Getting into my car and heading home on U.S. 101 was a major homecoming for me! Every mile traveled, every song on the radio, every minute of that trip, was eager anticipation.

The reunions almost made the goodbyes worth it.

There were times when I almost thought I was the lucky one. The pain of the weekly partings made those Friday homecomings that much sweeter.

And now I tried somehow to convey that thought to my friend Joe. "You've had a loss none of us have experienced," I told him. "But think what you have to look forward to! What a moment that's going to be when you and Matt and Jessica are together again!"

He nodded. "I couldn't have gotten through this week if I didn't believe that."

Later as we stood together at the cemetery and saw the casket lowered into the ground, I realized anew what heaven means to us. Reunions . . . and then no more goodbyes!

* * *

During my recent Bible land trip, our tour group noticed a cemetery with something unusual about it. It was surrounded by hundreds of tiny homes. For some curious reason, an astounding number of people wanted to live right next to the graveyard!

We asked the guide about it. "Oh, yes," he responded. "Many people believe that in the resurrection, this is where it will all happen. They live in those houses so they can be right here near their loved ones when that time comes."

I thought about that later and realized with a touch of irony that I had never before thought about the physical logistics of the reunions we have so long anticipated. Putting it bluntly: *How are so many of our family going to get from all corners of the globe to that little cemetery in St. Helena, California?* In all the commotion of the Second Coming, I don't suppose the airlines and bus companies will be running on a regular schedule.

Well, I didn't worry about that for long. As I worked on this manuscript, it suddenly came to me: A God who provides such elegant care for His children will surely arrange limousine service so that we can savor our treasured moments of meeting. *We will ride in chariots of fire just as Elijah did, with angels driving us wherever we want to go.* "St. Helena, please . . . and hurry! Please!"

Babies to their mothers' arms. Spouses reunited. Parents and children together again. And a reunion in St. Helena like you just wouldn't believe.

And then no more goodbyes. Never again.

EPILOGUE
Dennis's Dilemma

L eave it to Dennis the Menace to ask the really important questions.

He is on his way out of church one Sunday morning with his parents, Mr. and Mrs. Menace (or is it Mitchell?). As he reflects thoughtfully on the sermon and its theological implications, a look of frustration crosses his face. Finally he looks up with a plaintive question for Dad: "How am I gonna get to heaven if I don't get my wings till I get there?"

Many of us have been wondering the same thing ourselves. Not about the wings so much, but the underlying issue: *How do we get there?* What good is a book on heaven that doesn't give the directions?

That's the problem with every travel brochure. There's nothing wrong with the four-color pictures and breathtaking copy describing the waiting paradise. Lush golf course . . . memorable cuisine . . . three heated swimming pools . . . jacuzzis . . . color TVs in every suite. Enough already! I'm sold.

Just one thing: *Where am I supposed to get the money to go?* How do I get there? Answer me that, will you?

* * *

All through the Bible that question comes pounding through, expressed over and over by concerned would-be citizens of the better land.

Rich young ruler: "What do I do?" Jailer in Philippi to Paul and Silas: "What do I do?" The entire town of Nineveh: "What do we do?"

Even today you can ask that question and get a hundred different answers. The three parties just mentioned received these responses, in order: (a) keep the commandments—and sell everything you have and give to the poor; (b) believe in the

Lord Jesus; (c) put on sackcloth, call urgently on God, and give up your evil ways.

"What do we do?" Wheat or tares, sheep or goats, wise or foolish virgins, the mark of the beast or the seal of God? All of us would like to make the right choice in the end . . . when it really counts the most.

Every denomination has an answer. Indeed, every church has 10 different branches, or "wings," and *they* each have an answer as well. You almost can't tell the players without a scorecard.

I receive literature from the "cheap grace" people, from the works group, from the "God'll let everyone in" wing, and from the All Ten Commandments or Else! Subcommittee . . . and this is just in my own denomination. You're probably on a few mailing lists too.

What do we do?

I don't have every definitive answer, and I won't pretend that I do. All I can share is the good news that I do know, and here it is. In fact, two marvelous pieces of good news.

First of all, it is possible to get there! John 3:16 makes that crystal clear: "Whosoever believeth in him should not perish, but have eternal life." Jesus is coming soon to save *someone* . . . why not you and me?

Second, God tells us we can know we are in that group. First John 5:13 is a cherished Bible verse well underlined in my Bible: "I write this to you who believe in the name of the Son of God, that you may *know* that you have eternal life" (RSV).

I have wrestled with the question What do we do? No doubt you have too. I've read books, listened to nearly four decades' worth of sermons, prayed, and discussed the question with my many relatives who are ministers—and as you must realize by now, I've got a bunch of them.

Curiously, the more I hear and study and pray and listen, the shorter my "To Do" list gets. Has that been your experience? Day by day God is leading me into a quietly growing conviction that a short list is enough.

May I share mine with you? Accept it for whatever it may do

for you . . . and then keep praying and growing in your own journey.

1. Surrender your life to God.

2. Spend some time today getting acquainted with Jesus Christ.

3. Tomorrow, repeat Steps 1 and 2.

In parish after parish Morris Venden fixes his congregations with a penetrating gaze and then asks one pointed question:

"Are you spending time alone with God each day getting to know Him?"

That's it. That one urgent query is pretty much the sum of his ministry. Old Testament studies . . . hermeneutics . . . eschatology . . . Pauline epistles . . . all other worthwhile focuses take a back seat to that paramount question of friendship with God.

And many hundreds of men and women who have sat in his congregations and prayerfully read his books testify that their Christian life really solidified when they began to focus on this one thing.

At 6:15 in the morning I give my life anew to God for the day. I spend a thoughtful period of time reading about Him and fellowshipping with Him in prayer. I look for opportunities throughout the day to involve myself in service for Him on behalf of others.

Tomorrow I will do the same thing again.

It's a routine that has proved to be a tremendous blessing to me. I invite you to try it.

"Seek ye first the kingdom of God," Jesus advises. And I have truly found that all other things "shall be added unto you." Really.

Victory over besetting sins? Spend time with Christ each day, and temptations—sometimes slowly but always surely—will fade away.

Confused over God's will for your life? Spend time with Christ each day, and the answers invariably emerge.

Embroiled in religious politics or petty church battles? That quiet time with God every morning will bring a heavenly perspective to your down-to-earth dilemmas.

I've just finished reading Ralph Neall's *How Long, O Lord?* It's a wonderfully challenging study of the dilemma of Christ's delay in returning for His saints, and it eloquently answers the question "What do we do?"

* * *

Neall points to the often-overlooked fact that Matthew 24—the "Second Coming" chapter—is followed by three parables in chapter 25: the wise and foolish virgins, the servants and their talents, and the sheep and goats.

What's the message for us? he asks. What do we do in preparation?

1. Spend time with God each day. Draw upon His power. Get acquainted with the Bridegroom. (Wise virgins.)

2. Do the work God gives you to do where you are. Put your talents to good use in useful labor for Him. (Wise servants.)

3. Feed the hungry, visit the sick, clothe the naked, minister to those in prison, take a cold drink to a stranger. (Sheep.)

Neall concludes that whether Christ comes in 100 days or 100 years, you'll be ready if you're doing those three things.

And it all *begins* with that ever-growing friendship with Christ.

It's such an elementary truth that when Jesus comes again, He is coming to get His *friends.* Again, remember the Bridegroom and the ten virgins? "I know you not," He said sadly to the five left out in the cold night air.

* * *

I was looking for a simple conclusion to this epilogue, so I went to the obvious source: my young daughter Karli. Like Rev. D. T. Menace, she is a master theologian.

"Are you going to heaven?" I asked her one evening at bedtime.

She wrinkled her nose at me. "Uh-huh." She nodded without hesitating.

"How come you get to go?" I prodded.

"Because I love Jesus. Everybody who loves Him gets to go."

Out of the mouths of babes . . .

Are you getting to know Him? today? and tomorrow? and every day after that—right up until the day Jesus comes with a list of friends He's eager to spend eternity with in heaven?

Good. I'll meet you there soon.